BRANDED FOR CHRIST

EFFECTIVE EVANGELISM TECHNIQUES

ROBERT F. FELLER

WESTBOW
PRESS®
A DIVISION OF THOMAS NELSON
& ZONDERVAN

WestBow Press books may be ordered through booksellers or by contacting:

WestBow Press
A Division of Thomas Nelson & Zondervan
1663 Liberty Drive
Bloomington, IN 47403
www.westbowpress.com
1 (866) 928-1240

Because of the dynamic nature of the Internet, any web addresses or links contained in this book may have changed since publication and may no longer be valid. The views expressed in this work are solely those of the author and do not necessarily reflect the views of the publisher, and the publisher hereby disclaims any responsibility for them.

The Branding Iron-Cross was procured from Clipart on Openclipart. All Clipart on Openclipart are available for unlimited commercial use. Clipart may be used commercially for education, for church, for your job, or even to manufacture products globally.

Scripture quotations marked (NIV) are taken from the Holy Bible, New International Version®, NIV®. Copyright © 1973, 1978, 1984, 2011 by Biblica, Inc.™ Used by permission of Zondervan. All rights reserved.

ISBN: 978-1-5127-5391-2 (sc)

Library of Congress Control Number: 2016913662

Print information available on the last page.

WestBow Press rev. date: 10/21/2016

In loving memory of our daughter Michelle A. Nelson who was called home by her heavenly Father into the waiting arms of Jesus on Ash Wednesday, February 10, 2016, after a five-year battle with cancer.

"I have fought the good fight, I have finished the race, I have kept the faith. Now there is in store for me the crown of righteousness, which the Lord, the righteous Judge, will award to me on that day—and not only to me, but also to all who have longed for his appearing." (II Timothy 4:7-8)

CONTENTS

INTRODUCTION

I thought that before I take off my boots and riding chaps, remove the saddle, and put my mighty steed out to pasture, that I would pen this book.

It is true that both clergy and laymen have attended or taught courses in evangelism. This attempt is to apply a different style using a metaphor associated with the life of the American cowboy with evangelism. Cowboys, in the past, as well as in the present, play an important role in the life of America. I hope it will hit home to reveal some new techniques and helpful suggestions to not only to assist churches struggling to maintain an effective evangelism program, but to challenge them to greater heights. Possibly some of the techniques described in this book will place a burr under your saddle to spur you to do more in outreach. The Christian church must take seriously to reach out with the message of salvation through personal witnessing.

So often we reminisce about "the good old days". But how good were they? In the positive perspective we spent quality time with our family, meals were shared daily and we had long conversations. Negatively, we lacked modern communication technology such as the internet and social media; medical advances were slow and travel was not at the speed we know today. At times the church-at-large is caught up in old-fashioned methods of evangelism. These old ways do not work to reach the unchurched. New methods such as one-to-one relationships with a conversational tone must be in the forefront. It is imperative that the church develop a new format of evangelism to reach the *Nones, Busters, Boomers, Millennials, and Mosaics*. In Chapter

Two, "Different Brands," these categories will be discussed showing how the church-at-large may be an effective witness. Chapter Eleven, "Changing Scenes on the Prairie—A National Survey," describes how churches in Lutheran, Presbyterian, Baptist, Methodist and Episcopal denominations implement evangelism in church planning.

Congregations believe that they have to start all over by eliminating liturgy, creeds, and instruction. This is the wrong approach! Every denomination has a rich heritage that should be preserved at all costs. No, we do not do things for tradition's sake. Churches need to have a clear-cut vision, set realistic goals, be focused on Christ, and be a beacon in this dark world.

I hope that some of these evangelism techniques will enable members to be better equipped to serve their Lord. How do you do it? I invite you to read on. Truly we have been BRANDED FOR CHRIST, not with a burdensome stigma, but with the Holy Spirit's guidance to reach those who do not know Christ as their personal Savior.

May God the Holy Spirit, working through the Word of God, BRAND more people with the ownership of Jesus Christ!

CHAPTER ONE

BRANDED BY CHRIST

EARLY PERSECUTIONS

The early Christians in the First Century faced severe persecutions under Nero and Diocletian.

These Roman emperors required absolute allegiance and demanded that every citizen claim them as their god. In order to test loyalty, subjects were made to take a pinch of salt, pour it over a statue of the emperor and declare "Caesar is Lord." Those who failed to do so were persecuted severely either by being thrown into the arena with wild beasts, or burned on crosses outside of Rome.

A large percentage of Christians were faithful and did not succumb to Caesar. Yet, there was a group called "the lapsi" who denied their Lord and gave in to this terrible decision to worship Caesar. During these difficult times of persecution, Christians at first made the sign of the cross in the sand as they greeted everyone. They found that this was dangerous, for Rome had spies who turned in the Christians. As a result Christians had to develop an ingenious plan to not only recognize one another but to outwit the Romans. They did this by drawing the symbol of the fish or ICHTHUS in Greek which means Jesus Christ God's Son Savior. Our God has given us the blessing of His Word "Be faithful even to the point of death, and I will give you the crown of life." (Rev. 2:10)

MODERN WITNESSES

Christians are persecuted in subtle formats today. There is the ridicule, shunning, and avoiding of the Christian. This can be stressful for a Child of God. Our Lord desires that we articulate the faith. Have you been branded by the cross of Christ to witness to your Christian faith? God never said it would be easy. The cross brands us with the searing desire to tell others of Christ. This branding can be painful and may take various forms of testing by our Lord. Have you been branded by Christ? To the world our message sometimes falls on non-spiritual ears. We must testify to the hope that is within us. The Greek word MARTERIA (witness) describes not only those who were martyred, but encourages us to be living witnesses for Christ. Witnesses to a crime are important to a legal case in court. The prosecution has to produce its witnesses as does the defense team. All of the witnesses are cross-examined by both lawyers. Some witnesses perjure themselves and, if proven, may receive jail sentences for perjury. God wants us to be living witnesses for Jesus Christ.

A MARKED MAN

If there was ever a man who was branded for Christ it was Paul the apostle. "Finally, let no one cause me trouble, for I bear on my body the marks[1] of Jesus." (Galatians 6:17)

Paul endured stonings, beatings, shipwrecks and persecution for the sake of the gospel. His body depicts the scars of actual disfigurement. In Chapter 5 of Paul's letter to the Galatians he is responding to accusations the Judaizers are making against him. Their adage was that you must follow the Law of circumcision in order to be a Christian. Throughout Paul's epistles he condemns the Judaizers who followed the law. When the Judaizers viewed the scars and marks upon Paul they thought he had inflicted himself with his brand of Christ. Such marks were forbidden in the law. "Do not cut your bodies for the dead or put tattoo marks on yourselves.

I am the Lord." (Lev. 19:28). But Paul did not inflict these brands upon himself. The apostle bore these marks as a good soldier of Jesus Christ. When slave owners branded their slaves it meant they owned that slave and nobody dared interfere or try to gain ownership of that slave. Paul, in Gal. 6:17, attests to the fact that Christ owns him. To whom to you belong? Who is in control of your life? Too many people in the world pride themselves with the adage "I am in control of my life." Not really. In the Christian's frame of reference we belong to Jesus Christ. Just think of the number of times in a day we may use the word "belong." "I belong to that church," "I belong to this family," "I belong to this club." Scripturally, we belong to Jesus Christ. The word "belong" is used numerous times in the Bible. They include: "And you also are among those who are called to belong to Jesus Christ." (Romans 1:6) "If we live, we live to the Lord; and if we die, we die to the Lord. So, whether we live or die, we belong to the Lord." (Romans 14:8) "Those who belong to Christ Jesus have crucified the sinful nature with its passions and desires." (Gal. 5:24)

We see from the Scriptures the numerous ways Paul was branded for Christ:

1) BRANDED BY SUFFERING

Paul could say under divine inspiration, "I consider that our present sufferings are not worth comparing with the glory that will be revealed in us." (Romans 8:18) If there was any man that suffered it was the apostle Paul. Throughout his trials and tribulations, he exulted in Romans that the present sufferings can't be compared to the glory that awaits Christians in heaven. At times Christians lose their focus on Christ. Our goal is heaven through faith in Jesus Christ as our Lord and Savior. Many accept Christ as Savior, but how many also regard him as the Lord of their lives? We have been BRANDED BY THE MASTER to serve our master. People serve all sorts of masters—many are taskmasters demanding complete obedience. Christians have only one Master and that is Christ.

3

How are you enduring sufferings in your life? People moan and groan about their given situations. But are they justified? Sometimes. At times it gets hot in our individual and family furnaces of afflictions. The question is raised, "Why do the righteous suffer and the wicked prosper? It just isn't fair." God answers the prophet Habakkuk. "The righteous shall live by faith." (Habakkuk 2:4.) "Not only so, but we also rejoice in our sufferings, because we know that suffering produces perseverance: perseverance, character; and character, hope." (Romans 5:3-4.)

2) BRANDED BY ZEAL FOR THE LORD

Truly our Lord used Paul as his chosen vessel to preach the Word in season and out of season. Nothing could quench the zeal Paul had for his Lord. He had a Damascus experience where he became physically blind but later saw the light to be an ambassador to the Gentiles. We never know how our gracious Lord will use us in His kingdom. Sometimes we plan but God chooses a different path. Does the church-at-large have the burning passion to spread God's Word to every human being? Are we so selfish as Christians that we try to keep Christ only to ourselves? I hope not. May God the Holy Spirit so guide all of us and enlighten our hearts by His gracious visitation.

3) BRANDED BY DEDICATION

Paul knew the job that God had outlined for him. He received the Macedonian call. We may never receive a Macedonian call as Paul, but we are all called to be witnesses for Jesus Christ. Is the church committed to implement The Great Commission of our Lord? What motivates you to action as a Christian? Does it take the Holy Spirit to hit you between the eyes with a spiritual two by four? Do you get the hint? People spend most of their time on things that they love the most. Who do you love the most? Wife? Children? Grandchildren? Great-grandchildren? Of course God wants us to love all of these people. But foremost our love should be for Christ our Lord.

4) BRANDED BY HUMILITY

The devil uses pride as one of the tools in his toolbox to throw us off center and to become wobbly recruits in the army of Jesus Christ. "Pride goes before destruction, a haughty spirit before a fall." (Proverbs 16:18) "For whoever exalts himself will be humbled, and whoever humbles himself shall be exalted." (Matt. 23:12). God desires us to be humble witnesses to articulate the faith. Pride, arrogance, and obstinacy are tempting. One of the many ways we can be effective witnesses for Christ is to walk humbly before our God.

5) BRANDED BY LOVE

Paul was a servant of the cross. Throughout his years as an apostle he grew in the grace and knowledge of his Lord and Savior Jesus Christ. Our Lord desires that we grow not only in our love for him, but also for our fellow man. At times we have been wronged either by character assassination or false rumors. The forgiven forgive out of love (I John 4: 7-10). We, too, must be as indefatigable as Paul and be motivated out of love to reach out to everyone. Are you motivated by the love of Christ to spread his Word to the far corners of the world? The Holy Spirit prompts us and spurs us onward for our divine task!

NO APOLOGY FOR THE GOSPEL

The church must use and utilize apologetics. What do you mean? Many think we should apologize and compromise our Christianity! Not in the least. The word *apologetics* is derived from the Greek word APOLOGIA, a speech made in defense. Therefore apologetics is that branch of theology that treats of defending the faith. We do not apologize but defend the faith. The Apostle Peter in (I Peter 3:15) states: "Always be prepared to give an answer to everyone who asks you to give the reason for the hope that you have. But do this with gentleness and respect." Are you prepared to witness to your faith in Jesus Christ at all times? You may try to rationalize that it just isn't a convenient time to let the world know I have been branded by Christ to testify to the truth of the gospel. The Apostle Paul never made an excuse for the gospel. Paul states: "I am not ashamed of the gospel, because it is the power[2] of God for the salvation of everyone who believes: first for the Jew, then for the Gentile." (Romans 1:16)

I.D.

A brand on a cow denotes ownership. A brand on the ear of a calf marks the calf by the owner. Rustlers try to blot out an old brand by using a flat iron for a new brand. The devil wants to blot out the brand Christ has placed upon us through the cross and resurrection. He attempts this as The Great Deceiver" in many ways. They may include:

"You are not worthy to be a disciple of Christ."
"God could have chosen angels to do a better job as his representatives on earth."
"What will other people think of you?
"You are too fanatical about your faith."
"You do not have a good knowledge of the Bible."
"Forget it-- it's the preacher's job, not yours--to witness"
"You are too busy with your family, job, and work. You can't risk time witnessing."
"You have done this before and there is nothing new to learn."

LOSING THEIR HEADS

I have visited the footsteps of the Apostle Paul in Corinth. When visiting the museum at Corinth a docent points out that the beautiful marble statues of politicians are headless. What happened? They were very wise in ancient days: when the Corinthians carved a marble statue of a politician the head was changed when politicians changed.

In Corinth, Crispus the synagogue ruler, and his whole household believed in the Lord. God spoke to Paul in a vision "Do not be afraid; keep on speaking, do not be silent. For I am with you, and no one is going to attack and harm you, because I have many people in this city." (Acts 18:9)

BE A BOLD WITNESS

God the Holy Spirit will give us confidence to boldly witness as Paul did in Corinth and throughout his ministry. Moses, although a great leader for the Israelites, wasn't articulate. He complained to God "I can't speak; I will allow Aaron to speak for me."

Do you have a valid excuse for not articulating the faith? At one occasion Jehovah spoke to Moses in a burning bush. Tremendous.

BRANDING PRODUCES RESULTS

Branding is a chief nomenclature in the vocabulary of the cowboy. A certain brand seared into the flesh of the cow signifies that with this brand the particular animal is owned by him. Branding denoted ownership. All brands are registered in a brand book in every respective state where branding is done. The brand on cattle is the most effective means of identification. It is permanent.

We, too, have been "branded" indelibly by Christ to denote his divine ownership. As Christians we have been "branded" by his cross to denote that he and he only has the right of ownership over us. Yet we are servants, and not slaves for Christ as the world regards slaves. We do the Master's bidding and recognize His ownership in our lives, and yet we are free men and women in Christ. Christ has broken the shackles of sin that bound us.

SLAVE OR BONDSMAN?

The Greek word DOULOS denotes a slave in servitude to his master. In 1 Corinthians 7:23 the translation is "a person who gives himself to the will of another." A better translation is in Romans 6:17 where Paul refers to himself as a bondsman for Christ. We too were formerly in servitude to Satan, but through Christ's most precious blood, have become bondsmen for Christ. We are bound to Christ by the cords of his love as demonstrated by his death on the cross for the sins of the world. We now have a new Master, and that person is Jesus Christ.

Are you a bondsman for Jesus Christ? So often congregations, regardless of their denomination, declare we do not have evangelism boards or committees because every member is an evangelist. That is true in theory, but not in practice. Who is accountable? The Pastor should take the lead in all evangelism efforts in the congregation.

ANOTHER BRANDING

Persecution may be another form of being marked by Christ to the world. There are countless Christians in the world who have confessed Christ and been faithful to his Word and are now suffering martyrdom. At this time in the United States we do not suffer that form of persecution such as being beheaded or imprisoned.

But there is a subtle form of persecution in America which raises its tentacles in the work place and in the sport world. A football player was criticized severely by the news media for praying before a football game; Christians sometimes are deliberately overlooked for an office promotion because they are Christians.

UNWANTED

At Hot Springs, South Dakota you will see the federal sanctuary for horses. They number one million. These feral horses are branded with "U" denoting "UNWANTED". The horses are cared for either by feed lots or they run on the grassy plains for food. At intervals the U.S. Government will place these horses up for adoption. Similarly, people feel unwanted or neglected. No one is unwanted or neglected by our Lord, for our God demonstrates his abounding love to all, daily.

As evangelists we must show to the unchurched that they are loved by God and wanted by Christ. God wants to place his spiritual brand upon them. We, too, must show and radiate Christian love to show that we care about their spiritual welfare.

STAMPED

Travelers are required to possess a valid passport in order to travel outside the United States. At each destination the passport is stamped. As Christians we have been "stamped" by our heavenly Father with the cross of the forgiveness of sins that his Son purchased with his blood. But at times. as weary pilgrims traveling this earth, we become discouraged and frustrated in our evangelism efforts. As the forgiven, our Lord wants us to spread his love to those who do not know him. What an awesome task before us!

OWNERSHIP

As human beings we have the desire to own things whether it is an auto, home, or other possessions. Advertising specialists always attempt to create a need or desire to possess items. The ads claim, "You will be a better person, "a more-fulfilled person," or "you can have what your neighbor has." The ad men are highly successful in their campaigns. We needed to ask ourselves, "Do I need this?" In most cases we do not. Many families become "maxed out" on their credit cards; others go into bankruptcy.

We also have spiritual needs that often are not satisfied. Some people do not know what they want even in the spiritual realm. As evangelists we must pray that the Holy Spirit will give us numerous opportunities to witness when he creates that spiritual need in the hearts of men.

BOUGHT WITH A PRICE

The Apostle Paul reminds us "Do you know that your body is a temple of the Holy Spirit, who is in you, whom you have received from God? You are not your own; you are bought with a price. Therefore honor God with your body." (1 Corinthians 6:19-20) Christ purchased our salvation by shedding his most precious blood to redeem us from sin, death, and the power of Satan. We are therefore branded by Christ and bear the marks of Christ as the redeemed of the Lord. No longer are we in the servitude of sin, but in service to Christ the King of Kings.

But do our lives reflect that we have been branded by Christ? At times it does not. We all fail most miserably when we do not witness for Christ by telling others that they have a Savior.

TWICE MINE

Joey and his mother went to the local park to sail his newly-made sailboat. The little boy was content as his sailboat wafted across the lake. Then, suddenly, a high wind blew his sailboat out of sight. Both he and his mother searched the park for the lost sailboat. To no avail, it was lost. Joey cried and it was difficult for his mother to console her son. She promised to buy him a new boat. Joey refused, for he wanted to find his sailboat. They asked visitors in the park and even his friends about the sailboat. No one had seen it. Joey and his mother visited pawn shops in his city. One day his eyes lit up and he exclaimed to his mother as he saw his sailboat in the pawn shop window "There it is, mother, my boat!" When they had purchased the sailboat he exclaimed as he caressed the boat "You are twice mine--I made you and I bought you back."

"For you know that it was not with perishable things such as silver or gold that you were redeemed[3] from the empty way of life handed down to you from your forefathers."

(I Peter 1:18) Christ has redeemed us from sin, death, and the power of the devil by his holy blood that was shed on the cross. Jesus paid the ransom price to our heavenly Father with his life.

AMBASSADORS

Paul states, "We are therefore Christ's ambassadors as though God were making his appeal through us." (2 Corinthians 5:20) In 2013 the news was highlighted by ambassadors, consulates, and even the death of an ambassador. An ambassador[4] is one who represents his country on foreign soil. Actually, we are ambassadors for Christ on the foreign soil of the world that does not know Christ as its personal Savior. There must be a clear proclamation of the gospel. There are large cities as well as isolated outposts where ambassadors represent our country. So must we be ambassadors of the Word.

CHILDREN OF GOD

God is our heavenly Father through Christ. As earthly children place their trust and confidence in their father, how much more should we place our complete trust in our heavenly Father. We must say "Abba Father!" Our heavenly Father will never abandon us as earthly fathers may. We must more fully love our heavenly Father, for he guides our lives. John, the apostle of love, says, "How great is the love the Father has lavished on us, that we should be called children of God! The reason the world does not know us is that it did not know him." (I John 3:1)We should always go to our heavenly Father, not only in times of duress and problems, but also in good times to praise his name. "The Spirit himself testifies with our spirit that we are God's children." (Romans 8:16)

We, who were formerly spiritually abandoned by our sin, orphaned by our attitude, and unadoptable, have been adopted by our heavenly Father through the merits of Jesus Christ. We have a heavenly Father who deeply loves and cares for us. Our heavenly Father's plan is our eternal welfare. When he sees that his children are straying from the fold he divinely intervenes.

What kind of a child are you? Belligerent? Argumentative? Brusque? Reticent? Compliant? Trusting? At times we are not cognizant of the Father's love but we take heart in the Scriptures that state "And we know that in all things God works for the good of those who love him, who have been called according to his purpose." (Romans 8:28)

SALTY CHRISTIANS

Salt is an important ingredient in the diet of a human being. Too much sodium in our diets is risky and is a deterrent to our well-being. Labels on all food products list the amount of sodium contained in the products. But salt tastes good!. What would mashed potatoes be with without a touch of salt? What would that thick juicy steak be without a dash of salt? Jesus utilizes the term salt as a metaphor for Christians. Jesus says, "You are the salt of the earth. But if the salt loses its saltiness, how can it be made salty again? It is no longer good for anything, except to be thrown out and trampled by men." (Matthew 5:13) Salt flavors food and acts as a preservative but it must retain its potency to be effective. In ancient Egypt pyramid workers were paid with a salary of salt as it was a valuable commodity to the ancients.

What about you? Have you lost your saltiness as a Christian? Have you lost your desire to articulate the gospel? If you are losing your saltiness, go back to the Word of God and ask the Holy Spirit's guidance in the all-important task to seek the lost. Be a salty Christian although it does not come naturally. We must constantly be students of the Word and draw our daily strength and sustenance from it.

LIGHT OF THE WORLD

On a tour of the Holy Land in 2011, our guide pointed to a lighted hillside and commented that this is the hill Jesus referred to in Matthew 5:14-16: "You are the light of the world. A city on a hill cannot be hidden. Neither do people light a lamp and put it under a bowl. Instead they put it on a stand, and it gives light to everyone in the house. In the same way, let your light shine before men, that they may see your good deeds and praise your Father in heaven." Light is another nomenclature Jesus utilizes to emphasize the importance that Christians are the light of the world. Too often our lights have become dim and we fail to radiate the love of Christ to the world. Tarnished silver does not shine. But when it is highly polished it radiates with an untold sparkle. God wants us to polish our silver--our evangelism approach to the world. We may never say a word but our actions count. Love is contagious and is radiated by Christians throughout the world. Our nation has experienced great wildfires in the western portion of our United States that have devastated acres with a holocaust of flames. The Holy Spirit is a driving fire in the church. He motivates Christians to witness in a relational method to the unchurched. His fire is not devastation, but salvation through Christ. Never limit the power of the Holy Spirit in your lives!

U.P.O.B.

U.P.O.B.- What is it? To Christians it means The Universal Priesthood of Believers. It was Dr. Martin Luther, during the Lutheran Reformation, who stressed this forgotten doctrine. In Luther's sermons, teachings, and writings he emphasized this key doctrine of the Bible. Do we hear the message of this beautiful doctrine in our pulpits today? Not too often. It is a comforting, confronting, and challenging doctrine for all believers in Christ.

What does it mean? By faith in Jesus Christ as our personal Savior we do not need a human priest to intercede for us, for Christ is our divine Mediator and priest who offered himself up for our sins. In our lives of sanctification we love and serve our Savior. Listen to the words of the Apostle Peter, "But you are a chosen people, a royal priesthood, a holy nation, a people belonging to God[5], that you may declare the praises of him who called you out of darkness into his wonderful light." (I Peter 2:9)

A CHOSEN PEOPLE

The Israelites were a people chosen by God to glorify Jahweh but they failed most miserably by their repeated idolatry. Still, God loved them. Now, all Christians by faith in Jesus Christ are God's chosen people.

A ROYAL PRIESTHOOD

The Old Testament is complete in enumerating offerings that the priests were to make daily. All of these sacrifices pointed to one supreme sacrifice--Jesus Christ as our Great High Priest who offered himself once and for all. In the OT the offerings were repeated over and over.

No longer do we need a human priest, for Christ has fulfilled his heavenly Father's requirement through the death of his Son. Today we offer our time, talent, and treasure to God and flex our spiritual muscles to witness.

A HOLY NATION

The Jews had many laws to obey, such as Civil Laws, Ceremonial Laws, and Ten Commandments. Only the Ten Commandments are binding upon us today. The Israelites were disobedient and recalcitrant in fulfilling the concept of a holy nation. Only holy and blameless people will be allowed into heaven. How can anyone qualify? It is not up to us, for Christ died for our sins and rose victorious on the first Easter. By believing in Christ as our personal Savior we are counted as holy and blameless through the blood of the Lamb.

A PEOPLE BELONGING TO GOD

We belong first of all to our Lord and Savior Jesus Christ who gave himself upon the cross for our redemption. The price was high for our eternal salvation. If God dealt with us according to our sins, he would have every right to disown us as children are disowned and cut out of earthly wills. We have been made the adopted children of God by faith in Jesus Christ. Christ has placed his brand of ownership upon us. Christians are the treasured possession of God.[5]

What an incentive, motivation, and challenge to articulate our faith and praise our God for what he has done for us!

THE AZTECS

The Aztecs sold slaves at a price of 100 cocoa beans per slave. In ancient times life was cheap when many slaves were sold into servitude. Life is truly precious, so much more precious and costly in the sight of God who sent his only son to die for the sins of the whole world.

UNDER NEW MANAGEMENT

Restaurants close their doors for many reasons. These may include lack of interest in their food, high food prices, or poor management. The building will stand vacant until a new vendor occupies the space. If a new restaurant opens, the owner sends coupons to advertise in the newspaper and TV ads proclaim that they are now "UNDER NEW MANAGEMENT." As Christians, formerly under sin, we are owned and managed by Jesus Christ. Through the gracious operation of the Holy Spirit we have become new creatures in Christ. Paul states, "Therefore, if anyone is in Christ he is a new creature; the old has gone, the new has come!" (2 Corinthians 5:17)

NOTES

1 The Greek TA STIGMATA - "bear the marks, a mark burnt in a brand." The Judaizers, a group that required strict adherence to the law, demanded to see proof of compliance from Paul. It was common that slave owners branded their slaves. There were even incidents of criminals and soldiers that were branded. This did not apply to Paul. The apostle countered their attacks and said that he was branded by Christ.

2 "Power" in the Greek is DUNAMIS. The English word dynamite is derived from this word. The gospel is explosive and has the power to melt cold hearts. The Holy Spirit uses the gospel to bring salvation to mankind.

3 ELUTHROTHETE – "you were ransomed." The Greek word LUTROO means to release by paying a ransom price. This redemption was accomplished by Christ's crucifixion.

4 Greek translation is PRESBEUOMEN – "we are ambassadors," also "an elder, one who is experienced in the Word."

5 The Greek LAOS EIS PERIPOIESIN - "a people for his own possession." The Hebrew translation in Malachi 3:17 states, "They will be mine, says the Lord Almighty, in the day when I make up my treasured possession." In the LXX PERIPOIESIN denotes "my jewels."

CHAPTER TWO

DIFFERENT BRANDS

"Flanking" was another nomenclature utilized by the cowboy in branding. Cowboys worked together in a team. The "iron man," with a burning iron, branded the cow and the "tally man" recorded the brand, earmark, and sex of the calf. When the iron became too cold the "iron man" would call for a "hot man" to bring a hot branding iron. "Ear marks" were next.

No, not the type of pork hidden in bills passed by Congress, but brands to distinguish one cow from another. The brand marked ownership. The Western cowboy took great pride in correctly reading all of the complicated brands on cattle. The cow was branded for life.

How does the world read your brand of Christianity? Is it the pure unadulterated gospel of grace in the merits of Jesus or is it a different brand?

The American cowboy utilizes two types of branding, namely, Rope and Drag Branding and Table Branding. The Rope and Drag method is favored because it is easier to rope the calf by its hind legs and drag it to a branding area instead of lifting the calf to a surface for Table Branding. Equipment is also an issue in Table Branding. The cowboy has branding down to a science.

We can learn from this in dealing with people. We do not physically brand or injure human beings, but we must brand

Christians with effective training in order to articulate the gospel. Some would say in desperation, "Use any method, but do something!" Many churches in dire circumstances, and in exasperation, do just that and get into trouble. There needs to be recognition that old methods do not work and a fresh approach to evangelism is needed.

The church must strike while the branding iron of the gospel is hot.

LABELING

Some people check labels when buying groceries, prescriptions, or clothing looking for quality and quantity. Name brands are very popular. However, examining generic brand labels usually reveals the same ingredients as the name brand. Name brands often become popular because of immense advertising campaigns by manufacturers. Reading labels and checking expiration dates can result in big savings!

The unbeliever and the unchurched scrutinize the lives of Christians. This scrutiny motivates Christians to more effectively radiate the love of Christ. What kind of a label do you show to the world? Will your life label attract the unchurched or turn people off? Evangelism is not a chore or duty, but a privilege and joy, fulfilling The Great Commission Christ has mandated to his church.

WRONG AND CONFUSING LABELING

There was a housewife who organized her kitchen cabinets; she knew where everything was. But a guest in her house would be confounded by her system: she placed Salt in the Sugar and marked the container Sugar; Baking Soda in the Flour and marked the receptacle Flour; and Pepper in the Paprika shaker and marked it Pepper. Boy! Were people confused when they came to her house!

Do you as a Christian display the proper label? How does the world read your label?

BRANDED

The term "branded" is utilized in purchasing a used auto. The term means a used car that has been "branded" by another state and is revealed in the CARFAX report. Usually it means that an insurance company has declared it a total loss. Some costly antique furniture manufactured by Nerder Brothers has a unique branding burned into it.

We have a great God who has "branded" us as his people. Branding took days. It was arduous for cowboys and led to exhaustion. Cattle cringed when branding time came. To a cow the branding iron is an instrument of torture as hot iron sears the flesh. The branding was for a moment and then it was over.

Our Lord continues to touch our lives with his branding iron to test our faith and show a token of his love. Jesus says, "Come to me, all you who are weary and burdened, and I will give you rest." (Matthew 11:28)

SOME DISTURBING STATISTICS

The *Nones* are 60 million people, 20% of the US population who say they have no religious connection. According to the world population *Nones* number seven billion or 41% who do not know Christ as Savior. In 2015 a Pew Research Center article asked, "Nones, Are You Looking for a Religion that Would be Right for You?" *Nones'* responses were not encouraging: 88% said they were not looking, 10% were looking, 2% don't know. A 2012 poll by the Pew Research Center's Forum on Religion & Public Life revealed:

> 68% - **Believed in God, more than half of these feel a deep connection with nature.**
> 37% - **Were spiritual, but not religious.**
> 21% - **Prayed daily.**

These statistics are disturbing because they show that *Nones* are growing rapidly in the United States. Truly, the field is white unto harvest. What a challenge to the church! Statisticians have attempted to find the reasons for the increase of *Nones*. The pendulum swings from church involvement in politics to economics and intrusion of the secular world. Generational replacement also plays an important role in the increase of *None*.

SOME DEMOGRAPHICS

What role does demographics play in attracting the unaffiliated? According to a 2012 report from the Pew Research Center for the People & the Press, 63% of the unaffiliated declare that religion is losing its influence in the lives of people in America. They offer the following rationale:

+ The church is too concerned about money.
+ Too much a focus on rules.
+ The church's participation in politics.

While 77% state it helps the poor. In 2007, Robert Putman & David Campbell coined the term "luminals" (the unaffiliated becoming affiliated with a religious body). On the positive side 78% say that the church offers fellowship. Campbell, coined the term of "luminals" (the unaffiliated becoming affiliated.) Their research found that 10% of most major religious bodies are "luminals."

THE CHALLENGE TO THE CHURCH

Usually when *Nones* fill out a questionnaire on religious preference they list themselves as either atheist, agnostic, or nothing. As in all generations, there are groups in America that are less receptive to Christianity. Scripture states, "First of all, you must understand that in the last days scoffers will come, scoffing and following their own evil desires." (2 Peter 3:3) Some may say "I am spiritual." But what do they mean? We are all spiritual, for our Lord has given all of us a soul.

This is an exciting and challenging time in the existence of the church. Old ways of evangelism no longer work but the call to arms continues: Lift high the Cross! We have to return to the First Century Model of the early church, meeting in homes and speaking to people directly, using the "one-to-one" method.

ARE WE SELF-SUFFICIENT?

Nones consider themselves self-sufficient, needing no spiritual guidance. It is good to be independent, but in essence we are all dependent upon others in one way or another. "Not that we are competent to claim anything for ourselves, but our competence comes from God." (2 Corinthians 3:5) Jesus said "I am the vine, you are the branches. If a man remains in me and I in him he will bear much fruit; apart from me you can do nothing." (John 15:5) We are dependent upon the Lord and must rely upon him. People fail to realize that their greatest spiritual need is to be reconciled to God through the merits of Jesus Christ. The Holy Spirit convicts man of his sin and points him to a Savior. "For all have sinned and fall short of the glory of God." (Romans 3:20). "For the wages of sin is death" (LAW) "but the gift of God is eternal life in Christ Jesus our Lord." (GOSPEL) (Romans 6:23)

NONES' FALSE BELIEFS

Although *Nones* state that they are unaffiliated, they do have beliefs. They include: astrology, reincarnation, connection with nature in a mystical experience, and communication with the dead. All of these are contrary to the Scriptures! A large portion of our population has many misconceptions of Christianity. The United States is a vast mission field. Years ago, we sent numerous missionaries to the far corners of the world. Now, foreign missionaries are coming to evangelize America.

Where did we go wrong? The question always arises in the minds of the unaffiliated: "Is Christianity worth it and do I want to follow?"

OUTREACH TO *NONES*

What is the church's strategic plan of outreach to *Nones?*

+ Elucidate by example that Christianity is not a series of rules.
+ Emulate the love of Christ.
+ Tell them what Christ means to you.
+ Less stress on financial matters.
+ The church should not participate in politics.
+ Show that the church follows Scriptures by administering to the poor, widows, and orphans.
+ Invite them to fellowship gatherings (e.g. seminars, topic studies).
+ Demonstrate that you care about them (e.g. invite to neighborhood get-togethers and other functions).
+ Witness, starting with the Natural Knowledge of God and lead up to the Revealed Knowledge of God.
+ Lovingly point out false beliefs.
+ Build a solid relationship with the unaffiliated.
+ Invite them to a worship service and furnish transportation.
+ Do not argue nor browbeat.

MILLENNIALS

Within the large church denominations, eighty million *Millennials* (born 1980-1997, ages 18-32), formerly affiliated, are leaving the church. Only 58% of them claim that God exists. What changed their thinking? Could the church-at-large be guilty? Possibly. Maybe it didn't reach out when they had a spiritual need or they were ignored in church planning or we failed to listen to them.

Millennials are characterized by their technological know-how (e.g. Facebook, Instagram, Smart Phone, Internet, etc.) As a group they are well-educated with high IQ's; along with assertiveness they are optimistic and caring. Involved politically and liking challenge, they enjoy multi-tasking, team effort and volunteering. A large portion of *Millennials* did not grow up in a church-going family; instead they followed the pattern of their parents who did not attend church.

The Scriptures declare "Train a child in the way he should go, and when he is old he will not turn from it." (Proverbs 22:6) Too often we emphasize church attendance to the exclusion of a personal relationship with Christ. The brand of a Christian is to make a diligent use of Word and Sacraments (The Means of Grace).

OUTREACH TO *MILLENNIALS*

How can the church-at-large effectively minister to *Millennials?* Here are some suggestions:

+ Be involved in the community to demonstrate that the church is concerned about people.
+ Testify to personal experience with Christ.
+ Show genuine love for them.
+ Encourage *Millennials* to participate in Christian projects as related to the church. Volunteerism is one of the earmarks of this group.
+ Emphasize that biblical discipleship follows God's Word. Christians can exemplify a pattern for *Millennials*.
+ Stress that the church is a caring community.
+ Challenge with leadership training.

BUSTERS

Busters were born during an era (1965-1977) characterized by increased illegitimate births, single-parents, and high housing costs. A large percentage remained single, there was a rise in non-European immigration and the unemployment rate reached 7.1%. Most of those killed in the World Trade Center terrorist attack of 9/11/01 were *Busters*.

These factors precipitated apathy and cynicism but led to technological literacy and self-reliance. Moral truth became relative with an accompanying disrespect for authority. Thus, the family is viewed as dysfunctional and the influence of a church life non-existent.

OUTREACH TO *BUSTERS*

How can the church reach this generation?

+ Create dialogue sessions.
+ Plan small group discussions.
+ Assemble contemporary worship services.
+ Focus on less structure.
+ Formulate need-based activities.
+ Avoid decision-theology in coming to faith.

BOOMERS

Baby *Boomers* (1946-1964), known as "Generation X," presently constitute 76 million people. Positively, their brand marks include optimism. They have an excellent work ethic, are good team members in the workplace as they enjoy group decision-making. An orientation to specific goals includes a plan for imminent retirement, formulating trusts and wills, with health concerns and care for aging parents. Negatively, they have drifted away from the established church, having no concern for a religious life.

OUTREACH TO *BOOMERS*

Boomers have special brands: insight, vision, energy and initiative. These are useful in the church--they can get things done. Although leading busy lives, they still put their skills to work in the church.

What a spiritual arsenal to tap for God's Kingdom! Pastors can encourage and enlist these seniors to be leaders in the evangelism program of their congregations. One way to discover a *Boomers* gift for evangelism is to encourage a Spiritual Gifts Inventory. Results are usually enlightening and exciting.

MOSAICS

Mosaics (1984-2002) are distinguished as the youngest of the generations. What are their brands? They include a positive self-image and outlook on life; they tend to have close friends and seek new experiences; they are trusting of authority. To compliment an excellent education they exhibit concern about their community, seeking cooperation and teamwork rather than individuality to meet challenges.

OUTREACH TO MOSAICS

A large problem in outreach to *Mosaics* is an attitude of moral pragmatism wherein moral issues and life decisions are based on a "whatever works" philosophy.

The church must show that Scriptures reveal absolute truth and guides them evangelically to reach good moral decisions based on the Word of God. Discipleship must be used in guiding *Mosaics* to integrate their faith as they deal with issues. Without changing the gospel, new methods are required, creative ideas are needed. Above all, Christians must radiate the love of Christ in their personal lives in order to build relationships and serve as a friend to these teenagers.

LABELS ON GMO FOODS

Numerous nations and some states in the USA have GMO (Genetically Modified Organisms) labeling laws that have not been proven that GMO foods are harmful nor any better than other foods.

These labels can be complimentary or derogatory while informing the public that the food is special.

What is your label before the world? Do we as Christians portray a positive image of Christian life to the non-believer? Although we often fail, nevertheless God in His wisdom uses us to articulate the gospel to the world. Paul says, "You yourselves are our letter, written on our hearts, known and read by everybody." (2 Corinthians 3:2) The world labels us but God brands us to be witnesses of the gospel.

CRACKED POTS FOR CHRIST

The world sometimes calls Christians "*Crackpots*". But let us look at the term more closely.

One day a collector of relics brought a vase to a restorer because the vase was cracked. He told the clerk, "I want this vase replicated." He returned to the shop and was shocked that the vase had a crack in it. He argued with the shopkeeper, blaming him for the mistake. The shopkeeper's reply was "You ordered an exact replica of the original and I delivered the goods."

No, Christians are not "*Crackpots*," instead "cracked pots." We are all sinful human beings who have come short of the glory of God. He takes "cracked pots" and restores us perfectly through God, the Holy Spirit.

CHURCHED OR CHURCHLESS

Many books have been written describing the circumstances as well as the statistics of why various generations go to church or fail to attend. Clergy are often judged by attendance and the amount of the offering on Sundays. Although we are a society that clamors for statistics of attendance and offering, we may be asking the wrong questions.

It is not whether a person is churched or unchurched but what is the nature of their relationship to Jesus Christ. Once a firm faith is established through the power of the Holy Spirit, changes occur in the life of a Christian. Christ brands us as his own.

CHANGED PERSON

The Holy Spirit, through the Word, changes the heart of an individual. It is a transforming and divine intervention. Jesus says in The Beatitudes "Blessed are those who hunger and thirst for righteousness, for they will be filled." (Matt. 5:6) "I rejoiced with those who said to me, 'Let us go to the house of the Lord.' " (Psalm 122:1) As transformed people, there is a hunger and thirst to worship with God's family and become active members of a congregation.

BRANDING TERMS

The term "Maverick" denotes unbranded cattle with unknown ownership. The term "Orejana" denotes cows of an unbranded animal. The cowboy recognized and respected brands. A particular brand belonged to a specific ranch.

By faith we belong to Christ marked with the cross. During my ministry, one Ash Wednesday, after the Imposition of Ashes, I had a golden opportunity to witness at a grocery store when the checkout clerk inquired, "What is the meaning of the cross of ashes on your forehead?" I explained that the ashes not only depict our mortality, but also the beginning of Lent when we focus on the death and resurrection of Christ for our salvation.

Dust to dust, ashes to ashes. "Dust you are and to dust you will return." (Genesis 3:19)

THE REAL BRAND

The Brand Book is the cowboy's bible. It records all recognized brands. If a particular brand does not appear in the Brand Book, it is fraudulent. Rustlers try to disguise the real brand by adding or altering the known brand.

The world as a rustler attempts to alter the real brand of Christians, the cross of Christ. Instead, attempts are made to substitute fallacious brands, unknown in biblical circles. What is your brand? I pray it is always the cross of Christ!

THE BRAND THAT SAVES

As brands denote ownership, Christ has placed his spiritual brand of ownership upon the Christian. There was a king who drew a black cross beside some of those who were thrown into a dungeon. The captives saw the black crosses beside their names and exclaimed, "We are doomed to die by the gallows!" As the captives were marched into the courtyard where the hangman stood, the guard said, "When your name is called, step forward three paces." Six men stepped forward. Then the guard announced, "You have been pardoned by the king, you are free men."

We have been freed from the bondage of sin, death, and the power of the devil by the black cross of Calvary. But do we bask in this radiance? Do we reflect the cross of Christ in our daily lives? Do we witness to others about redemption through the blood of Christ?

OTHER BRANDS

The Western cowboy was quite creative in designing his special brand consisting of letters, numbers, and symbols. These are some of the different types used by cowboys:

+ Vent Brand means the original bill of sale and denotes that he is the owner.
+ Counter- Branding is a wrong brand that was rectified by re-branding.

28

- Road Brand depicts cattle branded during a cattle drive, used especially for those who have strayed from the herd.
- County Brand, utilized in Texas counties, shows a prescribed letter on the cow's neck, for each Texas county. If cattle changes ownership during a cattle drive there can be several brands burned into their hide.
- Running Brand consists of a straight poker used most often by rustlers. In order to rectify this abuse, a law has been passed requiring that a branding iron have a stamp brand.

Christ has placed his brand upon the Christian. The brand is clear and distinguishable. We blur the brand with our sin, neglect, and failure to effectively witness for Christ.

AN EXERCISE IN EVANGELISM

On a scale of 1-10 (10- highest; 1-lowest) rate the following methods of effectiveness in reaching out to prospects.

1) Door-To-Door Canvas _____
2) Area Prayer Walk _____
3) Pastor's Membership Class _____
4) Church Attendance _____
5) Bible Classes _____
6) Relational (one-To one) _____
7) Layman's Visit _____
8) Pastor's Visit _____
9) Personal Testimony _____
10) Phone Call _____
11) E-Mail Message _____
12) Seminars _____

RATING AN EVANGELISM EXERCISE

RELATIONAL (One-To-One) ranks number 10 as the most effective. Evangelism must be accomplished through relational evangelism by building a trust level with the prospect.

PERSONAL TESTIMONY ranks number 9. In order to give personal testimony, there must be a personal relationship with a prospect.

LAYMEN'S VISIT ranks number 8 on the scale. It has been proven that a committed and well trained lay person is very effective in articulating the Good News of salvation.

PASTOR'S VISIT ranks number 7 on the scale. Many pastors have the spiritual gift of evangelism and are effective; however, a lay person can be more effective because he can relate more readily to a prospect.

PASTOR'S MEMBERSHP CLASS is number 6 in effectively reaching the unchurched. This is an opportunity for pastors to inform potential members of salient biblical doctrines of the Word of God.

CHURCH ATTENDANCE ranks number 5 on the scale. Christians project a loving spirit by regular church attendance. This example can overcome indifference to the Gospel and open the door to inviting an unchurched prospect. Caution should be used before issuing an invitation.

SEMINARS rank number 4 on the scale. Inviting a prospect to a church seminar may possibly pique an interest to examine spiritual life.

BIBLE CLASSES rank number 3 on the scale. Christians have to be committed to study the Word of God. Prospects at the beginning of their spiritual journey do not have the hunger and thirst for Bible study.

DOOR-TO-DOOR CANVASS and PRAYER WALKS rank number 2 on the scale as they are ineffective. Both give the evangelist a false sense of accomplishment because they involve physical activity and a high degree of planning.

PHONE CALLS and E-MAILS are the least effective means of communicating with the unchurched.

CHAPTER THREE

SEND IN THE CLOWNS

What is a circus without clowns? Young and old laugh at the gimmicks and antics of circus clowns. There is even a school for clowns where they sharpen their entertainment skills. Clowns also play a vital role at rodeos throughout our country. Bulls are mean machines determined to toss the cowboy and injure him. Bring on the clowns! Rodeo clowns "distract" the bull so that he concentrates on the clowns, thus protecting the cowboy from injury.

Some congregations, thinking they will reach out to more people, substitute entertainment (clowns) instead of the pure gospel. This is a short-lived attraction which does not have staying power. It is a distraction from the spiritual role of the church.

DISTRACTIONS IN THE CHURCH

All churches are extremely busy with projects and activities. Christians delude themselves into thinking all of these activities are to the glory of God. The devil is the shrewdest Distracter in Christendom. He knows he has the ungodly within his control for he tells them he does not exist. Satan distracts the Christian in different ways: He whispers, "Don't hurry, you have plenty of time-missions can wait, evangelism isn't very important in the church." Another lie of Satan is "Who are you to speak the gospel? You are not worthy. You are too busy with bake sales, breakfasts, and all of your boards, how can you ever make time for evangelism?"

God issues an emergency mandate in the Scriptures: "I tell you, now is the time of God's favor, now is the day of salvation." (2 Corinthians 6:2) Some congregations allocate only a small pittance for evangelism in their overall church budgets. Isn't evangelism important?

RODEO CLOWNS

Rodeo clowns embody the art of distraction. Historically, rodeo clowns had their beginning around the 1900's when they were needed to entertain the public. In the 1930's barrels were introduced to protect clowns from the bulls. The clown became a "barrel man." Rodeos actually hired three men, two to act as bullfighters and the third was the clown adorned in an outlandish outfit to distract the bull. Cowboys, in rodeos throughout our country, compete in riding a bucking bronc. The longest ride wins a gold buckle plus cash.

The Christian has proverbial broncs to ride in his life of sanctification. The Child of God in his earthly pilgrimage faces unimagined hardships, disasters and sicknesses that can decimate him. We say with the Apostle Paul, "No, in all these things we are more than conquerors through him who loved us." (Romans 8:37)

DISTRACTED OR SERVING?

All of our churches have dedicated Christians with a great desire to glorify God and serve their Lord. But "distractions" often get in the way. Our Lord Jesus frequented the home of Mary, Martha, and Lazarus during his earthly ministry. Martha was concerned about providing a great meal for Jesus and she became upset when her sister Mary did not help her. "Lord, don't you care that my sister has left me to do the work by myself? Tell her to help me!" "Martha, Martha," the Lord answered, "you are worried and upset about many things, but only one thing is needed. Mary has chosen what is better, and it will not be taken away from her." (Luke 10:40-42) We are distracted in the church.

What place does evangelism have in your congregation? Often congregations are just busy with busywork. No matter how large or small a congregation, evangelism is a top priority. All pastors in every denomination are busy, but the lead MUST come from the Pastor. His blessing and leadership are needed for successful evangelistic outreach. "Distractions" are little things when compared to eternity.

DISTRACTIONS

The American Automobile Association (AAA) recently reported that drivers are highly distracted by driving while changing radio stations, sending and receiving email, and even using automated systems such as voice-activated phone. They termed these distractions "Inattentive Driving," which has triggered numerous auto accidents. It takes 100% concentration to drive an automobile. Some auto makers are addressing this situation in order to improve and ameliorate the causes of these known distractions. A more immediate danger is texting while driving. Distractions from texting and phoning while driving have led to disastrous auto accidents. Adults, as well as teens, fall prey to this bad habit.

When we view a horrific auto accident on the highway Christians may ask themselves, "Did the people who died in this accident know Christ as their personal Savior?" We think and wonder, but seldom put our witnessing into action. The Great Distracter, the devil, tempts us to veer from our course of action and blinds our focus on Christ. Most distractions lead us astray while still others affect our zeal for Jesus.

The devil certainly attempts and many times succeeds in distracting the Christian from the work of evangelism. How many times have all of us have made paltry excuses for not articulating the gospel message? Although there are many demands in life, we often fail to prioritize our goals.

BUSHWHACKED

Satan, as a fallen angel and smarter than any human being, attempts to "bushwhack" the Christian. He lays in ambush when we least expect it. He employs the moment of surprise or when we are discouraged to make us distrust God. "Be self-controlled and alert. Your enemy the devil prowls around like a roaring lion looking for someone to devour." (I Peter 5:8)

CLOWN COLLEGE DEGREES

Some congregations in the United States have established a Clown Ministry to train their members to administer to patients in hospitals as well as in nursing homes. There is always a place for good wholesome humor to cheer a weary soul. This ministry has been effective across the country in children's hospitals. Clowns, as we know from circuses, possess funny red noses, walk in floppy shoes, make funny noises with horns, and maneuver crazy cars around the center ring. It makes one laugh. There are all sorts of college degrees that a person may achieve in their lifetime. We are well acquainted with such degrees as M.D., DDS, STM, DD, JD, PHD, LLD. But how would you like to complete the requirements for a BCS[1]? Each congregation has to determine if a clown ministry is feasible and effective in their respective community.

CLOWN MINISTRY

Hospitals and nursing homes are filled with people not only facing a crisis in their lives, but may be at the point of death. Many are lonely, distressed, and despondent. Caregivers, such as physicians, nurses, chaplains, and family try to bring cheer. This is where The Life in Christ Circus, started in 1977, in St. Petersburg, Florida by Dr. Dick Hardel[2] has ministered to thousands of patients in care facilities throughout the United States and the world. This ministry stresses the theology of the Cross of Christ and helps people to see the love of God in their lives as well as bringing the healing power of laughter.

NOTES

[1] BCS is a Bachelor of Clown Science degree offered by Indiana University at the University Clown College since 2012. Core curriculum includes such courses as Make Them Smile, Make Them Laugh, Make Them Cry. Electives include Pass the Seltzer, A History of Clowning Props, Its Top Laugh: Clowning Through the Ages. Students can become CSPS—Licensed Clown Science Practitioners.
Clown Ministry and Wellness, Wellness, Clown Ministry, & Faith Formation, 2015.

[2] Dr. Hardel has, for decades, trained Christians to witness to their faith in Jesus Christ by being trained in the theology of clown ministry. Dr. Hardel modeled his Christ Clown College after Ringling Brothers, Barnum & Bailey Clown College. Students completing 60 class hours plus 35 hours of practice and performance time receive a diploma. Class subjects of Christ Clown College include Clowns' Image of the Mind of Christ, Christ is the Center of Christians Clowns, Clowns Open People to the Bible and many more biblical topics.
Clown Ministry and Wellness, Wellness, Clown Ministry, & Faith Formation, 2015.

CHAPTER FOUR

DANGERS ALONG THE TRAIL

PERILS ALONG THE WAY

As we ride our own dusty trail of life the path becomes clouded and unknown. Along this trail we will encounter a myriad of problems when we want to spread the gospel. The church is living in an era which is frustrating and challenging. America is apathetic, disinterested, and indifferent to the message of salvation. Churches trying to cope with the world offer entertainment during church services, instead of biblical worship. It is a cafeteria-type religion which allows you to pick and choose what you want from the Bible. Thomas Jefferson, a deist, cut and pasted his own bible choosing only those items he found pragmatic and ethical in Jesus' teachings. It is known as The Jeffersonian Bible and a copy is given to every person in Congress. Many think that presenting spiritual pabulum instead of the real meat of the Word is fulfilling the role of the church.

The Latin "Carpe Diem", seize the day, has great meaning in evangelism. We should "seize the day" everyday as another opportunity to spread the gospel. There are many opportunities to help prospects, such as furnishing transportation to the doctor or hospital, furnishing a meal, or simply giving a kind greeting.

CIMARRON

To the cowboy the word "Cimarron" defined an area that was wily or unruly. Congregations also face a "Cimarron" from time to time where there is disagreement, conflict and unruly behavior.

Failure to face the problems leads to disillusionment, resulting in ineffective outreach.

SAVED BY A FOG

Carl was a salesman who sold men's accessories in the Midwest. Before leaving for an early morning appointment in Des Moines, Iowa, he listened to the morning news. The weatherman reported that heavy fog had rolled in during the night. Carl was anxious about his appointment but felt sure that they would understand why he was detained. Subsequently Carl learned that there had been a 12 vehicle pile up on the highway that morning resulting in many injuries. God in his wisdom detained Carl in order to spare his life. When we are faced with spiritually foggy days that detain us, God protects us along our trail.

CROSSING A SWOLLEN STREAM

Cowboys have to take the lead and direct a herd when there is a roiling stream to cross. This requires careful planning and a cool head to prevent an emergency situation. A good method is to have a lead steer that will lead the cattle across the waterway. But what if the cattle balk and will not move even with a lead steer? The procedure is for the cowboy to take a small group of cows and force it into the water. He gives his horse the lead and loosens the bridle. Another cowboy urges a second group into the water, riding alongside on the downstream side to keep the cattle from drifting. When they have reached the other side, the rest of the herd is easily led across until the entire herd has crossed safely. Cattle will not cross a stream if they cannot see the other side which is a situation fraught with danger if they are blinded by the sun. Thus, a cowboy needs to carefully plan the timing of a crossing.

In evangelism there are numerous "roiling waterways" that prevent spreading the gospel.

Just as a cowboy has a method to deal with emergencies, the church-at-large confronts crises that can make spreading the gospel a daunting ask. Contrary to the cowboy' method of forcing cattle, Pastors must gently guide their people across the swollen rivers of life.

As cattle fear the water, so Christians have fear of witnessing. The devil capitalizes on this by stirring fear, pointing to uncharted waters and saying that words will fail the Christian as he talks of the good news of salvation through Christ Jesus. Fortunately, God has promised that the Holy Spirit will put the proper words into our mouths.

Lutherans, as a denomination, have been very hesitant in past years to venture forth fearlessly. In the past we waited until other denominations had a format which we then tried to replicate. Today, thank God, this is not longer true.

SOUTHWEST MONSOONS

During monsoon season in the Southwest, arroyos become swollen by turbulent rains rushing from the mountains. Only one foot of water can float a large vehicle downstream. Locals sometimes bypass safety barriers and are swept away. Rescue teams are employed to save them. Violation of the bypass can cost as much as $2,000.

DON'T GET STUCK

Gopher holes cause injury to cattle when they step in them. Cowboys protect their cattle from this pest by using a pressurized machine which eliminates gophers in their holes.

The devil creates spiritual gopher holes for Christians in order to impede their witness. As a fallen angel, he strikes when we are least likely to be aware of his subterfuge. He tries to put barriers, walls, and stumbling blocks in our paths. Are you vigilant? "In addition to all this, take up the shield of faith, with which you can extinguish all the flaming arrows of the evil one." (Ephesians 6: 16)

FIRE DANGERS

The American cowboy, from time immemorial, faced fire danger on the open range. The challenge of a prairie fire was that it threatened not only their lives, but that of the herd. One protection on the open range was a "back-fire," (starting a new fire in front of the one burning), thus containing the fire and stopping its spread. Another method was to create a fire guard, plowing furrows about 50 yards long, four furrows to a "set."

An interesting phenomenon was "foxfire," phosphorus light playing upon the ears and horns of cattle during a lightning storm.

Similarly, in the church, fires (gossip, conflict, innuendo) may break out. Containing the fire is necessary to prevent its becoming a holocaust. In these situations we have a system called "Matthew 18:15-17," which includes the steps directing the reconciliation procedure for individuals and the church.

Speak to the offending person.

If not successful, take another witness and speak to them again.

If he refuses to listen, tell it to the church.

The keys to success are love and patience, allowing sufficient time to put out the fire.

Satan is active and surrounds us with temptations and allurements. He desires to "sift you as wheat" (Luke 22:31) in the process. We must arm ourselves with the whole armor of God which Paul describes in detail (Ephesians 6: 10-17) Dressed in this spiritual armor we can fight the fires and be victorious.

BLIZZARDS

October 20, 1913 was catastrophic for ranchers in America. The Atlas Blizzard was sudden. Ranchers in western Wyoming and western South Dakota lost 75,000 head of cattle, a devastating blow. Just as sudden blizzards are crippling to some areas in the United States, so also the lack of evangelism planning hamper a congregation.

RIDE LINE

Stray cattle often drift away from the herd. These cattle are called "Windies." The term is used by cowboys to denote the exhaustion of cattle, horses and cowboys after driving cattle out of canyons and onto the plains. "Ride Line" is a term which describes the job of rounding up cattle.

Just as cowboys had to possess endurance and perseverance, so too the evangelist strives to develop outreach skills. The easiest thing to do is give up. Christians often do this, failing to endure and persevere in outreach.

RUSTLERS

Another danger on the prairie is rustlers who try to steal cattle by using counterfeit brands. Diabolically, they throw sand in the eyes of the young calves so that the calves cannot see to find their mothers. They then wrestle them to the ground and obscure their brand by adding to its design. Rustlers utilized insidious methods to purloin cattle. They employed such methods as:

1. Cutting of the ear to hide a telling earmark 2. Using a running iron to forge brands 3. Using acid to remove hair in order to counterfeit a brand 4. Stealing a neighbor's calves, rebranding them after altering the registered brand.

The rustling technique of Satan is to obscure the basic teachings of Christianity by introducing false doctrine and evil ways present in the world. Lucifer, the fallen angel of light, attempts all sorts of nefarious ways to tempt and allure, leading Christians to succumb to his wiles.

CIRCLE THE WAGONS

Early pioneers heading West in wagon trains were farmers seeking land. They were plagued by one obstacle after another—difficult terrain, Indian attacks, hunger, thirst, disease. The role of the wagonmaster was to get these hardy souls to their new homes where they could plow and plant. If there was perceived danger from attack, the command was, "Circle the Wagons!" This was a better defense than single wagons standing in a line. Pioneers fought valiantly, usually warding off attacks although on occasion an entire wagon train would be wiped out. Indians were resourceful attackers. They utilized their skills in horsemanship and archery to shoot fiery arrows into the cloth coverings of wagons forcing fighters into the open. Pioneers used the power of prayer when attacked by Indians, for they were people of great faith.

Spiritually the church-at-large has to "circle the wagons" when confronted by ongoing attacks from Satan. The American Indian was cunning and resourceful. Similarly the devil shoots his fiery arrows of temptation against the Christian in order to defeat him and be lethargic in his attitude toward outreach. The Pastor as "Wagonmaster" must direct the fight against his onslaughts and deadly blows energizing the congregation.

CHAPTER FIVE

FENCE STRADDLING OR REPAIRING FENCE LINES

THE FENCE-CUTTER'S WAR

In 1862 Lincoln passed the Homestead Act which allowed settlers to farm 160 acres for 5 years after which they owned the land. The West was still an open range. There were no barbed wire fences, cattle roamed freely. There was conflict because the farmer and the cattleman disagreed on who owned the land. In 1880 the situation turned nasty with the emergence of a Range War.

Cattlemen accused the farmers of rustling cattle. When fences were constructed, cattlemen cut them down. Intensifying the situation in 1880, at Sweet Water, Wyoming, there was a scarcity of beef on the market due to a 90% herd loss for cattlemen amounting to 100 million dollars in today's economy.

Ella Watson was a courageous woman who took a firm stand against the cattlemen during the range wars. She and her husband were hung by cattlemen for interfering with their business.

In 1883 the situation became even more intense, erupting in the Fence-Cutters War. There was fence cutting, destruction of property and even hangings of the farmers by cattlemen. Enmity, trickery and warfare were the result of political calumny during that era in the West.

Think of the spiritual warfare for our souls as Satan fights against us. In our former sinful state we were enemies of God. Now, by the grace of God and faith in Christ as our personal Savior, we are at peace with our heavenly Father. Satan continues to battle us for our souls; however, we do not go into this battle alone for "God is our Refuge and Strength, an ever present help in trouble. (Psalm 46:1)

In the West today, land where cattle once roamed is now occupied by homes. Even without fences, people can be "fence straddlers" in a spiritual sense due to indecision about spiritual matters. It is no longer necessary to use barbed wire to divide the land between neighbors. But there are spiritual fences to the gospel message. Only the Holy Spirit can remove spiritual fences between non-Christians and Christ.

The Holy Spirit guides us to cut down fences which are barriers that separate non-Christians from the gospel. Ask yourself whether you rely on the Holy Spirit when you give a Christian witness.

SPECTATORS OR PARTICIPANTS?

The Western cowboy coined the words "Op'ra House" to denote a cowboy sitting on the top rail of the main corral. He was there as a spectator watching other cowhands busting a bronc or training a horse.

In the church-at-large there is a spiritual locale for "Spectators Only." It is a comfortable place but does not spur us on to effective witnessing. There are several accounts in the Scriptures that talk about fence sitters on the top rail of life looking down on their fellow man. "Elijah went before the people and said, "How long will you waver between two opinions?" (I Kings 18:21) Spiritual indecision is no decision at all. "Whoever acknowledges me before men, I will also acknowledge before my Father in heaven. But whoever disowns me before men, I will disown before my Father in heaven." (Matthew 10:32-33). Are you sitting on the top rail being only a spectator, looking down on the sinful condition of non-Christians? Are you watching while others are working? God's commission to us is that we must boldly confess Christ to the world.

FALSE RELIGIOUS VIEWS

Cafeteria-style depicts the pick-and-choose type of religion. It is like eating at a buffet that offers all sorts of foods at the culinary delights. You can choose the food you desire and ignore the rest. So it is with a Cafeteria-style in modern America-pick-and-choose what you want for your religion. Today, the general populace has the attitude of "I can't be bothered with Christianity." We have to do everything in our evangelism arsenal to promulgate the gospel of Christ. We must exult Jesus Christ is Lord! "And every tongue confess that Jesus Christ is Lord, to the glory of God the Father." (Philippians 2:11)

Resistance to authority. Since the '60s there has been a great wave of rebellion against all types of authority. There is the disobedience of children, the union strikes, rebellion against civil disobedience. This resistance to authority has shown the pejorative spiral that is taking place in our churches.

Pluralism. This states there are all sorts of beliefs. How is your religion better than mine? This is a real avenue for an open door to witnessing.

People seek spiritual solace and desire an anchor of hope. They are looking for answers to life's problems at the same time shunning "membership" in churches, equating it with "commitment." And yet the Scriptures demand commitment. "Commit your way to the Lord; trust also in him and he will do this." (Psalm 37:5). As Christians we must be indefatigable in spreading the Word of God to benighted souls. Jesus says, "I am the way, and the truth and the life. No one comes to the Father except through me." (John 14:6)

BOX CARS OF DEATH

During the Nazi regime of World War II, when millions of Jews were hauled in box cars to the gas chambers of the death camps, some Jews felt a ray of hope as they passed churches along the railroad lines. They cried out in desperation, "For God's sake, help us!" All the German churches situated along the railroads secured a time table to determine when the box cars would pass their churches. What did they do? They played the organ louder and sang their hymns more lustily in order to drown out the cries of the Jews entombed in the box cars. The Germans were hypocritical Christians as they watched those Jews being transported to Dachau, Auschwitz, Treblinka and Buchenwald.

We, like the people in those German churches, ignore opportunities all around us for witnessing. We rationalize "Why, it isn't my job to tell others of Christ, let the clergy do it; my job takes all my energy, God knows I have to provide for my family; I don't feel motivated and I know they would tell me to mind my own business; my time is not my own; I can't be concerned about the spiritual welfare of someone else." We are endlessly creative in inventing excuses for not witnessing.

Do you ignore a roof that is leaking? Do you ignore polybutylene pipes that burst and have to be replaced at a cost of $6,000? Do you ignore your child who was involved in a terrible auto accident? Of course not, we are speedy in rectifying those situations. But we ignore the desperate plight of the non-Christian who doesn't know Jesus Christ as Savior. These people are as needful of our witnessing as those Jews in Germany, or as your child in an accident. People without Christ as their Savior today are in spiritual box cars headed to Hell.

We must be proactive in our evangelism effort.

STONE SOUP

Have you ever heard of it? It isn't advertised, nor is it in grocery stores. But it has a history. Years ago a group of villagers boiled a pot of water and threw in a stone. While the stone was boiling other villagers stopped by and asked, "What are you making?" "Stone soup," was the reply. "Let me add my carrots," said one person. Another said, "I want to throw in some potatoes". Other villagers added meat and herbs. The pot boiled and Stone Soup was invented.

In evangelism we have to pique curiosity and make the evangelism presentation interesting as well as biblical. The story of Stone Soup teaches us that we can accomplish great things for our Lord if everyone makes a contribution.

REBUILDING THE WALL

Nehemiah's name in Hebrew means "The Lord Comforts." He was a Godsend to his people after the Babylonian captivity when the Lord directed him to rebuild the walls surrounding the temple in Jerusalem. The task was not easy. In fact it was a dangerous job every day for him and his men to build a section of wall as their enemies attempted to tear it down as quickly as it was built.

Frustrated, but not deterred, Nehemiah pushed on with his dedicated crew of workmen. (Nehemiah 4: 6, 13-18) Eventually, for protection, the workmen armed themselves. In spite of their primitive tools the job was completed in 52 days. It was a miracle blessed by God, and God directed it. Nehemiah prayed, obeyed and took action.

What about us in the 21st century? Do we have the faith, courage, and determination of Nehemiah to channel our energies into useful avenues of evangelism? Nehemiah was an encourager. We must be encouragers, not only encouraging our people to be trained in evangelism, but to encourage the unchurched.

How do we do it? Nehemiah had a plan. Does the church-at-large have a plan to promulgate the gospel of Jesus Christ? Various polls indicate that some congregations, regardless of their size, have a lackadaisical attitude toward evangelism. We too, as Nehemiah, have to rebuild the walls that surround our faith. These walls are under attack by Satan.

Christ, by his death, broke the barrier of sin that had separated us from our heavenly Father. When the thick temple curtain was torn asunder as Jesus uttered, "It is finished!" our eternal salvation was completed and then sealed by his glorious resurrection. God uses modern day Nehemiahs to stand up for the truth amid spite, scorn, and ridicule. Don't allow the enemies of the cross to defeat us, but let us show faith and always build upon Christ the Chief Cornerstone in our lives!

DRIFTING

"Drift fences," constructed near the outskirts of a ranch, are deathtraps for cattle during severe blizzards in the West.

There are Spiritual fences that entrap people. For example, in taking an alcoholic to a bar, we can cause a brother or sister to fall from faith by placing a barrier in their way causing them to drift from the faith. Why do people drift away from Christ and the church? The devil places fences before us, such as: peer pressure, excessive concern with worldly allurements, our sinful flesh, and the church's failure to reach out.

SPIRITUAL URGENT CARE CENTERS

Churches must be spiritual Urgent Care Centers in the world. The church-at-large needs to ask relevant questions of the unchurched: what are the spiritual needs and how can the church meet these needs? And, specifically, what is a person's relationship to Jesus Christ? Once all these questions are answered, the process of witnessing can begin.

Many people in a poor economy declare bankruptcy. The four types are Chapter 7, Chapter 11, Chapter 12, and Chapter 13. It takes years to recover financially and rebuild credit worthiness. Yet many more people in this world are spiritually bankrupt. They do not have the riches and guarantee of salvation. Fortunately the church stands as a spiritual urgent care center, offering recovery through the blood of Jesus Christ without waiting years.

PENNILESS OR WEALTHY

A businessman lost his wealth in the stock market crash of 1929. He dismissed his employees and locked up his building. Driving home, these words resounded endlessly in his mind, "I am penniless--I am ruined." When he arrived home his 5-year old daughter heard him repeat them aloud. She climbed on his lap and asked "Daddy, what does it mean to be penniless?" "It means, honey, we do not have any money to buy items." She returned, handed him a penny and said, "This will make everything alright." When he rebuilt his department stores, he encased his daughter's penny as a charm and always wore it. Employees would ask him "Boss, what is the meaning of that penny when you are worth millions today?" His reply was, "That penny means so much to me and reminds me of when I was down and out and 5 year old daughter gave me hope and courage to forge ahead."

Oh, what riches we have in Christ! In our former state we were bereft and spiritually poverty-stricken; now, in Christ, we are spiritually wealthy. In fact, Christians are the wealthiest people (spiritually) on the face of the earth. God always takes care of his own in crises and traumatic situations.

NO COMFORTABLE CHRISTIANITY

A "Comfortable Christianity" has overflowed into the total fabric of many churches who do not take evangelism seriously. This kind of Christianity has no stresses, dangers, risks or challenges and there is no element of sacrifice or commitment. It is very pleasant to develop spiritual lethargy and fall into a "hammock of neglect"

Nowhere in Scriptures does it say that being a Christian would be easy and comfortable. Not at all. "We must go through many hardships to enter the kingdom of God." (Acts 14:22) Did Jeremiah, Elijah, Ezekiel, Daniel, Hosea or Paul and others in the Bible have a comfortable Christianity? No, but it was filled with stunning excitement and God-pleasing challenges.

When a frog is boiled in lukewarm water he feels quite comfortable. Then the cook turns up the heat and the frog boils to his death. Lukewarm Christians, like the frog, are comfortable with the status quo, having no intention of jumping out of their comfortable zone into an "uncomfortable" zone. Our Lord at times motivates us to become uncomfortable with our status quo and moves us forward in our outreach.

FOLLOW THE DIRECTIONS

Parents, with great ingenuity, hurriedly assemble toys when their children are young. Often they say to themselves, "This is easy, I don't need to read the directions." Then they arrive at a juncture where they are stymied; either they run out of parts or put the wrong bolt in the wrong place. Now they are forced to read the directions.

At times we are like those parents with respect to evangelism. We go off on our own tangents without a plan, or not being trained, and wonder why our outreach efforts are not working. GM, Ford, Chrysler, GE, Amana and practically all corporations offer comprehensive job training for all their employees. They realize that well-trained employees are more productive. So it goes with evangelism. We do not have to make up our own directions for our gracious God gives us the blueprint in his Holy Word. The Bible is the blueprint we must follow in order to be successful.

AVOIDANCE OR MOTIVATION

There are times when congregations fail to come to a common goal in their decision-making, creating conflict, which then leads to confusion of purpose in goal setting. Conflict, if not dealt with, will fester, decay and debilitate a congregation's efficiency. There are 4 ways to deal with conflict: 1) Avoidance 2) Accommodation 3) Collaboration 4) Negotiation. Avoidance is least effective while collaboration is the most effective. Instead of facing the need for evangelism, churches may take the avenue of avoidance.

A very large congregation in the Mid-West contracted a carpet company to lay hundreds of yards of carpet in their church. While they were laying the carpet, Polly, the parrot of the Pastor's wife, flew under the carpet creating a bulge. The Pastor's wife, searching for the whereabouts of Polly, asked the workmen "Have you seen my parrot? "They replied "No," as they crunched Polly under the carpet. Finally, the great day arrived when the congregation planned to rededicate their sanctuary with the new carpet. The members who arrived were thrilled. "Beautiful," "Great," "W should have done this long ago." But there was a distinct odor of rotting flesh. Members sniffed" "Iff" "Iff." It was Polly's entombed body, rotting away under the carpet.

Similarly, avoidance, a tendency to "sweep things under the rug," ignores the facts and realism of outreach. Congregations procrastinate with outreach in numerous ways: 1) WHEN we have enough time, 2) WHEN the church budget permits. 3) WHEN we have enough members interested in evangelism. 4) WHEN the Pastor will take the lead in evangelism. WHEN never comes.

AN EVANGELISM EXERCISE

The following are congregations who are heeding the mandate of The Great Commission of our Lord, while the others are not. Figure out the future of these congregations.

1) Our Master, Minneapolis, MN, is a congregation of 2,000 communicants and is 100 years old. Only 6 Pastors have served them in their history. The church also maintains a day school of 200 students. Attendance at the 4 worship services

is above average and every year they fulfill their budget of 2 million dollars. The congregation relies solely on "transfers in" and they have no concern about the changing community around them. How do you diagnose their future?

2) Galilee Lutheran, St. Louis, MO, is a small congregation of only 100 members located in a growing area of St. Louis County. The Pastor, a fervent evangelist, trains and equips his people in regular courses in evangelism and makes calls with his group every Sunday afternoon. What is the future of this congregation?

3) Transfiguration Lutheran, San Diego, CA, is an affluent suburban congregation of 1,000 members. There are no missions, no evangelism, no love for members or area, lukewarm and straddling the fence. What does Revelation 3:14-22 say to them?

4) Concordia Lutheran of San Antonio, TX, was a mission congregation with 64 members 64 years ago. Today it numbers 6,000 and has had a day school since 1998. What happened?

5) Coral Ridge Presbyterian of Fort Lauderdale, FL, started in 1959. Today, it has a membership of thousands. What happened?

NOTA BENE: Only Concordia and Coral Ridge are actual congregations. The other three are pseudo names of congregations.

Refer to Matthew 28: 18-20. What is Christ's mandate to the church? How is your congregation fulfilling The Great Commission?

SOME INTERESTING STATISTICS

What single item or combination of factors motivate individuals to seek out a church home? How bad do life stressors have to be before they seek spiritual help? Where do they go for the Balm of Gilead? The following are some of the emotional stressors that may motivate people to seek spiritual assistance. The Lutheran Hour Ministries and Lutheran Church Extension Fund Religious Survey of October 2002 have listed the following stressors:

Death of a loved one	51.8%
Health crisis	26.9%
Stress	25.8%
Family crisis	23.2%
Emotional crisis	22.5%
Friend/relative needed help	20.3%
Looking for direction in my life	20.2%
Financial crisis	19.1%
Marital crisis	18.0%

AN EVANGELISM EXERCISE

1. Which items constitute a vibrant personal testimony?

2. Explain the barriers to developing an effective evangelism program for a congregation.

3. What are the benefits of utilizing relational-style evangelism?

4. Why is training and practicing so important in evangelism?

5. Discuss the following: Obstacles to evangelism and How to overcome those obstacles.

6. Explain the following terms: HATCHED, MATCHED, DISPATCHED

7. List the venues of evangelism in your congregation and comment if they failed or succeeded.

8. Why are the "NONES" difficult to evangelize? List some of their false concepts and how to effectively witness to this group.

9. Discuss these terms: Children of God (I John 3:1) Ambassadors (2 Cor. 5:21) Salt of the Earth (Matt. 5:13) Light of the World (Matt. 5:14-16) Priesthood of Believers (I Peter 2:9)

10. What does this expression mean? "The church that fails to evangelize will fossilize."

11. Discuss the following Greek words and their important emphases in evangelism:
a) APOLOGIA b) ICHTHUS c) MARTERIA
d) DOULOS e) DUNAMIS f) EUANGELION.

CHAPTER SIX

GOOD ROPING or SLIPPERY LASSOS

THE DONT'S IN SLIPPERY LASSOS

1. DON'T BEGIN WITH "ARE YOU SAVED?" "DO YOU KNOW JESUS?"

These questions, as well as similar questions, backfire in the witnessing process because you put prospect on the spot and off guard. Evangelists may have used this terminology in the past, but these terms do not work today. Your hearer will turn you off and it will be difficult to speak to your prospect in the future.

2. DON'T INVITE TO WORSHIP SERVICES INITIALLY.

We should not immediately invite a prospect to a worship service for they may associate "church" with a negative experience of the past. Building a one-on-one relationship is the first step. An invitation to worship is most beneficial when there is trust.

3. DON'T ARGUE OR DEBATE RELIGION

Arguments about religious denominations and beliefs are counter-productive. There are some people outside the realm of Christianity who love to argue and debate religious questions. They delight to "snooker" a Christian into arguing. Arguments will not bear fruit.

4. DON'T USE THE FEAR OF PUNISHMENT.

It is a mistake to use punishment as a club to spiritually browbeat a prospect. This often happens when we become so persistent in our zeal that we press for a conversion. Bearing in mind that it is entirely the work of the Holy Spirit that converts people and our job is to speak the word of God's grace. The Holy Spirit works through that Word.

The early church was faced with those who advocated synergism. Greek, (*Syn*, together; *gero*, to work). Those who espoused this false doctrine said that God is at one end of the spectrum and man at the other end. They believed that it was a 50-50 situation where God and man meet halfway and man had to co-operate with God. This we know is false for God the Holy Spirit reaches down to man 100% without the co-operation of man at all.

5. DON'T QUOTE A LOT OF BIBLE VERSES.

At times we become verbose in quoting Bible verses to the point of overwhelming the prospect. Use Bible verses sparingly and at the correct time. Timing is important.

6. DON'T EXHIBIT A "BETTER THAN THOU" ATTITUDE.

You may have been a Christian all your life from the day of infant baptism; you came up through the spiritual ranks. God calls people at different times of life.

Jesus, in the Parable of The Workers in the Vineyard (Matthew 20:1-16) cites workers called to work in the field at different hours. Although they were employed at different hours, all received the same remuneration. In human terms an employee today would cry out "unfair working conditions and pay." This is a parable--an earthly story with a heavenly meaning. There is a danger to make a parable to walk on all fours (pressing every detail) to the point of demythologizing it. There is one point of comparison in every parable. God calls people to faith at different times of their lives.

7. DON'T BE CONDESCENDING TO THE OTHER PERSON AS A KNOW-IT-ALL.

No one person knows everything about evangelism. A good way to start is with the idea, "What new technique or approach can I learn today in order to be more effective in reaching another person with the "Good news?" Be motivated, but humble.

8. DON'T USE DOCTRINAL TERMINOLOGY.

Doctrinal terminology such as Sanctification, Soteriology, and Eschatology are foreign to the prospect. If you use those terms you confuse and may lead your prospect to think you are showing off your Christianity. Avoid embarrassing them, for there is the possibility that they have not had religious training or that their family was not affiliated with a church.

9. DON'T USE FEEL- GOOD CONCEPTS OR WATER DOWN SIN.

We are living in an era where television evangelists espouse a "feel good" religion—being a Christian is to "feel good" about it. They minimize sin by defining sin as "man's mistakes." The attitude that pervades is that everyone makes mistakes.

Sin in the Bible is defined as the breaking of God's Ten Commandments and that sin separates us from God. Mankind sins against God in thought, word, and deed. Man must repent and seek forgiveness in the blood of Christ.

10. DON'T GIVE UP IN EXASPERATION.

There are times when we are tempted to throw up our hands and say "What is the use? I have planted the evangelism seeds, but I don't see the fruit." Hold on! We, as Americans, are impatient people who desire instant success in everything. Evangelism can be a slow process and you may never see the fruit of your labors. There are times when we wish to give up on that situation where we spent so much time witnessing without result. The answer is to focus on Jesus who says. "I am the Vine, you are the branches. If a man remains in me and I in him, he will bear much fruit; apart from me he can do nothing." (John 15:5)

We are tempted to quit like the salesman, who tried to sell a dress suit to a man at a menswear store, using a "T-over" or "Turnover" technique. He turned the customer over to another salesman to see if he could cinch the sale. We are tempted to use "T-overs" in evangelism when exasperated and discouraged.

11. DON'T MAKE THEM FEEL UNCOMFORTABLE.

Maybe your witnessing is overbearing to the point of being pushy. Watch out! Here is where the trust level is essential. In the setting of witnessing, you and your prospect need to be comfortable. You don't want them to squirm trying to avoid you.

12. DON'T EXHIBIT INSINCERITY.

If you witness as if it is your duty, you exhibit insincerity. This lack of integrity is obvious to your prospect and you are labeled a "phony." Be genuine in your approach.

13. DON'T USE COMMUNITY CANVASSES.

Church canvasses were in vogue many years ago. Using that method, you asked only a few questions in order to either revisit the family or create a profile of the prospect. Actually, it was barely scratching the surface. On return to the church, the evangelism team would pat themselves on the back and say, "We covered this area with 500 calls; we accomplished our job." This was unproductive and is no longer used by a church looking for real results from evangelism. The one-to-one personal, conversational contact is always best.

14. DON'T USE A SHOTGUN APPROACH.

There is the danger of a shotgun approach in evangelism when a church tries to cover as much territory or persons as possible in the shortest period of time. Instead, try the rifle approach which centers on one person at a time to spread the gospel.

15. DON'T BE A PESSIMIST.

Sometimes evangelists become pessimists by looking on the dark side of witnessing.

It is easy to become so empathetic to a prospect's crises in life, that their burdens become yours. Instead, concentrate on the good news you are bringing and the prospect of joy instead of sorrow. Christians are optimists.

THE DO'S OF GOOD ROPING

What does a cowboy need to be proficient in roping? Roping gloves, excellent quality rope, a specialized saddle, a well-trained horse, and piggin' string. Roping gloves are manufactured of nylon, cotton or leather while ropes are manufactured of cotton, polyester or Cactus. Cowboys must have an excellent rope in order to be a contender on the rodeo circuit. Roping saddles are made with the best leather that is available. True craftsmen design these unique saddles as the horn of this special saddle acts as a cushion in order to absorb the weight of the bull. They are usually covered with beautiful graphic designs.

A rope is attached to the saddle horn while the cow is in motion. In good roping there must be head horses and heel horses. Head horses are used to zero in on the cow, while the heel horse is trained to stop on a dime. A tie-down horse is trained to work in tandem with the cowboy. The Piggin' string[2] is utilized in rodeo contests.

Let our lasso of the gospel sing the joy with the message of forgiveness in the blood of Christ. May your rope sing, not sting! All of the above equipment is essential to the cowboy in order to win gold buckles at rodeos. Can we as Christians do less in equipping ourselves to do good roping, instead of using slippery lassos in our witnessing?

GOOD ROPING TECHNIQUES

The following are some good roping techniques in evangelism:

1. DEVELOP A ONE-TO ONE RELATIONSHIP WITH A PROSPECT

We live in an age of smart phones and computers, using all sorts of ways to communicate like Twitter, Snapchat, Instagram. All of these methods have their respective place in everyday living but they can never replace the personal touch. For example, if you share pizza and beer with friends while the TV is on, there is little conversation. Likewise, checking your email or texting stops communication instantly if you are with friends. We seem to have lost the personal touch.

There are countless people we meet everyday who may be hungry for the Word of God and are prospects for witnessing. We see people at grocery stores, barber shops, the mall, auto stores, department stores, post office, bowling, special events--the list is inexhaustible.

Each day when you awake do you offer a prayer "Lord, this day direct someone to me that I can witness to and tell them of Christ's love."

2. USE PRAYER

Prayer is an essential part of our spiritual life. As human beings we rely too much on ourselves rather than on the mercy and guidance of our Lord. Prayer is the life breath of the child of God. Allowing time each day for prayer is essential. Everyone is busy in this hectic whirlwind world we live in. Young families with children are especially caught up in the warp of the time crunch. But no matter how busy our schedule, there needs to be time for prayer.

Prayer is a guiding light when we want to articulate the gospel to other people. It has been said, "Life is fragile, handle with prayer." All the greats of both the Old and New Testaments were men and women of prayer. The Scriptures state: "Be joyful always; pray continually; give thanks in all circumstances for this is God's will for you in Christ Jesus. (I Thessalonians 5:16-18) "The prayer of a righteous man is powerful and effective." (James 5:16b)

3. USE THE SCRIPTURES

We must daily be students of God's Word. Although we have heard and studied a familiar portion of the Scriptures, there is always opportunity to glean new truths from the Bible. "I have hidden your word in my heart that I might not sin against you." (Psalm 119:11) God's Word should be a hidden spiritual arsenal in our lives. Children in confirmation class sometimes complain about the amount of memory work as catechumens. They usually appreciate those verses they committed to memory when they are adults. Memorizing scriptures is not a static matter. Whatever our age, committing a Bible verse to memory every week or even every day increases our knowledge of the Bible.

Many of our servicemen imprisoned in the "Hanoi Hilton" POW camp remembered Bible verses they had memorized. They were greatly comforted and, as a result, their endurance in captivity was strengthened.

It is a discipline not only to read God's Word daily, but to memorize Bible passages. Has your memorization of the Scriptures grown since your confirmation days? Only when we know the Bible can we in turn communicate God's Word to other people. "All Scripture is God-breathed and is useful for teaching, rebuking, correcting and training in righteousness, so that the man of God may be thoroughly equipped for every good work." (2 Tim. 3:16-17) Scripture is not man-made, but divinely inspired by the Holy Spirit. A good witness has to know what they believe in order to clearly articulate the gospel.

4. THE HOLY SPIRIT'S GUIDANCE

It is easy to minimize the work of God the Holy Spirit in our lives. The Holy Spirit guides, enlightens, sanctifies, converts and strengthens our faith all while furnishing spiritual gifts and fruit of the Spirit to his people. May our prayer be when we witness to another person "God the Holy Spirit give me the knowledge to speak your Word of salvation to this person and may these words bear fruit in their lives. Empower me to speak this message of God's love. I ask these petitions in Jesus's name."

5. GET TO KNOW THAT PERSON

As human beings we are quite selfish. We must be concerned about other people, especially those who do not know Jesus as their personal Savior. In the past evangelism was hampered by a set format or an evangelism "kit." Witnessing needs to be natural and flow from our hearts. Probably the most difficult group to witness to are our own family and friends. We know them and they know us. It is easier to witness to a stranger. But without knowing their spiritual needs, your witness may be of limited value. Getting to know your prospect first allows you to address their spiritual needs, thus effectively paving the way for a better outcome of your witness. Why should you get to know and witness to another person? We do it because Christ shed his most precious blood for their sins also.

6. BE EQUIPPED THROUGH TRAINING

Everyone requires training in pursuit of their life's work. An autoworker requires training for the assembly line, a computer operator requires skills for their art, a physician requires years of study and residency, an engineer requires an engineering degree and a teacher requires a teaching degree. If training to develop life skills is vital how much more so it is for Christians to avail themselves of training in evangelism. This is where a Pastor needs to assume the role as chief trainer in evangelism.

When I served a congregation of 700 and a day school of 150 in the Midwest I conducted a course in evangelism every Sunday morning. Every Tuesday evening 8 of us, including the vicar, would call on first-time Sunday visitors. Additionally, every team had a cold call area to visit if they completed their assigned calls. We would reconvene that evening to recap the dynamics of our calls.

7. THE POWER OF PERSONAL TESTIMONY

Your personal testimony counts. The most effective witness is when you relate your personal experience of how Jesus came into your life and the difference his presence has made. It must be simple, short, and to the point. Tell the prospect about your life before Christ and then relate how Christ changed your life when he became your personal Savior.

Personal testimony reflects our background as a person. For some it may be a riotous life as a prodigal son or daughter. But probably most of us became the children of God on the day of our Baptism. Several members of my evangelism board have given their personal testimonies during worship services. Personal testimony reveals that we also are sinners in need of forgiveness on a daily basis in our lives.

It brings out the mortality of our flesh. We do this in the profession of our faith. "Let us hold unswervingly to the hope we profess, for he who promised is faithful." (Hebrews 10:23)

8. FOCUS ON CHRIST

What is your goal in life? Is it wealth, power, advanced education, an excellent retirement? Goals are necessary and have their respective place in our lives. But if we are narcissistic, self-indulgent, and sinful in our pursuit, we lose our focus on Christ.

S - self
I - I
N - nothing

Paul was fulfilled in his life when he said, "For me to live is Christ and to die is gain." (Philippians 1:21) We know that the things of this world will rust, decay, fade and become of no consequence in comparison to our heavenly home. And yet God has placed his Christians on this earth for a purpose, namely, to glorify God. "Do not store up for yourselves treasures on earth, where moth and rust destroy and where thieves break in and steal. But store up for yourselves treasures in heaven, where moth and rust do not destroy, and where thieves do not break in and steal. For where your treasure is, there your heart will be also." (Matthew 6: 19-21)

What is your priceless possession? I hope it is Christ. In witnessing, always focus on Christ. There are distractions all around which deter us from our quest. When we focus on Christ in our witnessing, remember "Let us fix our eyes on Jesus, the author and perfecter of our faith, who for the joy set before him endured the cross, scorning its shame and sat down at the right hand of the throne of God." (Hebrews 12: 2)

9. DEMONSTRATE CHRISTIAN LOVE

We are living in a sometimes loveless and thankless society. The word "thank you" is not heard often enough. This is evident when individuals receive gifts. Very few send a personal thank you. These personal notes are meaningful. Many Christian parents have trained their children at an early age to pen "thank you" notes, inculcating them with the spirit of gratitude. Christians in the First Century made a significant impression upon the people of their day when the heathen remarked, "See how they love one another." This type of love is missing today. The Greek language has three different words for love, while English has only one that can be modified by adjectives and adverbs. The Greek words are eros, philos, and agape.[1] Christian love can be demonstrated in many ways, for example, by taking meals to a home when there is a death in the family; by giving a brochure listing relevant Bible verses; by praying; by furnishing transportation; by hospital visits.

Tour groups visit Catacomb Domitta (Catacombs) of Rome where early Christians were buried. In the courtyard there are the Christian symbols CHI RHO, "Jesus the Good Shepherd;" ICHTHUS (fish) which translates "Jesus Christ God's Son Savior." Due to the fierce persecutions of Nero and Diocletian, Christians worshiped underground. Early Christians did not live in the catacombs, but rather buried their dead and held agape love feasts there.

10. BUILD A TRUST RAPPORT

Building a trust level with prospects is very important. We must trust other people until they betray our trust and then we have to be on our guard. A good friend may convey a confidence to you that should never be repeated to another human being. If you betray that confidence, you could lose a friend or a prospect. Our most important concern, of course, must be in Jesus Christ, as our personal Savior.

The Scriptures have countless verses dealing with trust. "Those who know your name will trust in you." (Psalm 9:10)

11. CONSIDER THEIR SPIRITUAL BACKGROUND

When we meet people, we do not know their spiritual background. Some people drift from the established church, others never had an affiliation with a church. There is a temptation to blurt out "Where do you go to church?" Although many Christians are members of both the visible and invisible church it is difficult for the non-Christian to fathom the invisible church. The mark of Christians is to avail themselves of the Means of Grace in their lives. This nurtures and edifies the child of God. Our chief concern for the prospect is their relation to Jesus Christ and that they are of the communion of saints. By having conversations with prospects we can determine where they are in their relationship to Jesus Christ. Don't be critical of the lack of a spiritual anchor in their lives for some never received Christian nurturing as children.

12. TIMING IS IMPORTANT

The American cowboy competes in local rodeos throughout the United States. But the big time is the Western States Ranch Rodeo Association National Finals. You have to be fast, precise, accurate, and teamwork. is required. Teams consisting of four men ply their skills in branding, tie down steer roping, rustler trailer loading, and sort-and-rope doctoring. The four-man team plies their skills in a famous event called trailer loading. As cattle enter the arena, the team has only four loops and four minutes to rope the steer, load it on the trailer, and shut the gate. Time is of the essence.

Timing is important in witnessing for Christ. There are situations in life when you may only have a short time to witness about God's love: at an airport while waiting for a plane connection, aboard an aircraft, on a travel tour. The message needs to be clear and not garbled. It is that God loves them, Christ died on the cross for their sins, and by faith in Christ as their personal Savior they will inherit eternal life.

13. OVERCOME YOUR FEAR AND TIMIDITY

Many church members have a repugnant attitude toward evangelism. Either they dismiss it as the preacher's job, or they are contented when the church body grows through people transferring in from other churches, or they simply do not care about the unchurched.

Evangelism teams experience fear: of rejection, of the unknown, of not being accepted, the fear of physical harm. Motivated by this fear which is Satan's work, they may say a silent prayer, "Lord, I pray this family is not home tonight." Fear is paralyzing, because Satan hovers and the correct words and answers disappear. When we are fearful and discouraged take to heart the words of David the psalmist, "The Lord is with me; I will not be afraid. What can man do to me?" (Psalm 118:6) God desires the Christian to be bold and courageous in articulating the gospel. A hesitating, milquetoast demeanor does not inspire confidence in your witness. Paul encouraged young Timothy as he faced numerous odds in the churches. (2 Timothy 1:1-14)

"When I called, you answered me; you made me bold and stouthearted." (Psalm 138:3) John and Peter, after boldly witnessing and confessing Christ to the Sanhedrin prayed, "Now, Lord, consider their threats and enable your servants to speak your word with great boldness.' (Acts 4:29) There are spiritual battles to be waged. We may lose some of the battles but we won't lose the eternal spiritual war for God is on our side.

14. BE HUMBLE

No one appreciates a person who is arrogant, selfish, and narcissistic. People extol their accomplishments, their stock market success, or wealth in worldly goods. There are many millionaires and even billionaires. Worldly wealth does not necessarily mean spiritual wealth.

It is different in the Scriptures, for it attests to rich men such as Abraham and Job who were physically very wealthy and also giants of faith. We need them today. Are you a wealthy person? Not in earthly wealth, but are you wealthy spiritually? We are all admonished by the Scriptures: "Pride goes before destruction, a haughty spirit before a fall." (Proverbs 16:18) "Humble yourselves before the Lord and he will lift you up." (James 4:10)

Are you blessed with spiritual gifts? Give all praise, honor, and glory to God for them!

Are you using these spiritual gifts to the glory of God? No one has all spiritual gifts. In order to spread the gospel, God, in his wisdom, gives all gifts necessary within a congregation.

As you witness, a prospect senses excessive pride, stubbornness, and an attitude of having all the answers. Instead, take for your example our Lord Jesus Christ. "And being found in appearance as a man, he humbled himself and became obedient to death---even death on a cross!" (Philippians 2:8)

15. BE SUCCINCT

There is a danger of being verbose in our witnessing. We may think that by presenting a detailed plan of salvation we are more effective. Not so. People are busy today. Be alert to the attitude of your prospect. By the Holy Spirit's direction, be awake and receptive to the Gospel. The bottom line is that God loves you. In the Bible, God made simple the way of salvation. Jesus said of himself, "I am the way, the truth, and the life, no one comes to the Father except through me." (John 14:6). You have sinned. Christ died and rose from the dead for you. Sin separates us from God. This barrier has been removed through the blood of Christ. Believe that Jesus Christ died for you and he is your personal Savior.

Salvation/conversion is God the Holy Spirit working directly on the hearts of people. The Holy Spirit produces changes in the hearts and lives of people. "Godly sorrow brings repentance that leads to salvation and leaves no regret, but worldly sorrow brings death." (2 Corinthians. 7:10)

16. NURTURE THE PROSPECT

Nurturing and edification are essential to the spiritual life of the new Christian. As we need certain nutrients in our bodies to sustain our earthly lives, nurturing is needed in the spiritual life of the new prospect. We can do this with prayer and encouraging words. Perhaps attending a worship service is not possible but the small home Bible class could be effective. All of us in our spiritual pilgrimage need edification and encouragement. Greek OIKODOME means the act of building and is in the Bible to denote edification, (of building up people in the Lord.) It takes patient work and prayer to direct new prospects as they grow in their faith.

17. IT TAKES COMMITMENT

We must be committed to telling others of the love of God in Christ. There was a member of a church who visited her pastor. As she told him what should be done in the congregation, the Pastor was patient and listened to her new programs for him to implement. He asked her, "All of these programs are fine--will you commit to helping with some of them?" "Oh, no," said the woman, "I am too busy with other commitments of Garden Club, bridge, and luncheons. I just do not have the time." Unfortunately, we are all familiar with by-standers and back-seat drivers who offer all sorts of advice but are woefully short of zeal for the work of the church.

18. DEVELOP GOOD LISTENING HABITS

Therapists are good listeners; we should try to emulate their skill. A prospect who talks about himself and his life wants to be heard.

Learning to be attentive, not interrupting or over-talking, is not only good manners, it allows time for introspection and for posing questions and comments. Often we respond too quickly and in our haste blurt out the wrong comment or answer. It can be very effective to simply listen. Scriptures record numerous verses concerning listening. "Let the wise listen and add to their learning, and let the discerning get guidance." (Proverbs 1:5) For the most part individuals like to unburden their hearts to you once trust is established.

19. DEMONSTRATE ZEAL AND EXCITEMENT

There is passion and excitement for Christians in the greatest message to be told to the world.

The 1st Century Christians, amid fiery persecutions under Nero and Diocletian, promulgated the gospel. Truly the blood of the martyrs was the seed of the church. When Constantine became emperor and Christianity the state religion things changed for the better. Constantine wasn't always a Christian. On the day of the battle against Maxentius, Oct 28, 312AD, on the Tiber River leading into Rome, Constantine and his army saw a message in the sky, an "X" (Greek for CHI RHO) meaning "Christ" and the Latin words "In Hoc Signo Vinces" or "with this sign, you will conquer." Maxentius was defeated and a day later Constantine marched victorious into Rome. Later he and his mother Helena established Christian churches and Constantine the Great proclaimed Christianity as the state religion. Paul the Apostle gives Christians words of encouragement, "Never be lacking in zeal, but keep your spiritual fervor, serving the Lord." (Romans 12:11)

20. RELATE THE URGENCY OF THE GOSPEL

Satan whispers lies and falsehoods in Christians' ears, attempting to dilute the Word and discourage the telling of it. One of his great tricks that has conned many Christians is "This world has stood for a long time, there is absolutely no urgency to spread the Gospel." Too many churches have allowed themselves to fall into this trap and do nothing in evangelism. When they do, some assume a lackadaisical attitude towards outreach.

Hospital emergency rooms as well as Urgent Care facilities have been established in most communities to deal with critical and urgent medical cases. What would happen if you needed urgent care on an emergency basis, only to discover that all of the emergency rooms and urgent care facilities in your city were closed? Great angst and trepidation would result.

What if churches closed their doors and especially their hearts to the souls who are spiritually dying? Time is of the essence and urgent care is needed: "I tell you, now is the time of God's favor, now is the day of salvation." (2 Corinthians 6:2)

21. BE CREATIVE IN ARTICULATING THE GOSPEL

The Patent Office is always inundated with requests for patent rights from the endless numbers of creative people in the United States. And there are companies that assist individuals who want to turn their creativity into a patent. Countless inventions are born out of creativity or by accident. One example is the white out we use to blot out writing and typing errors. It was created by accident, when secretary, Bette Nesmith Graham invented Liquid Paper in 1951.

The Christian, as well as the church, has to be creative in presenting the message of salvation to the world. I hear you saying, "I am not a creative person." I bet you are. In different venues of life we become creative by necessity. Your style for the presentation of the gospel is creative--for it is you that develop your own particular presentation.

22. BE AN ENCOURAGER

A Christian is an optimist. Numerous persons in the non-Christian world struggle with insurmountable problems and they do not know where to go for relief. Christianity has the answer. When we come into contact with the lonely and discouraged, one way to start the witnessing process is to offer a good word such as, "God's blessings in your work," "May the Lord bless your endeavors," "Make it a great day!" The Scriptures are replete with encouragement. "But let us encourage one another and all the more as you see the Day approaching" (Hebrews 10:25b) "For everything that was written in the past was written to teach us, so that through endurance and the encouragement of the Scriptures we might have hope." (Romans 15:4) "When Apollos wanted to go to Achaia, the brothers encouraged him and wrote to the disciples there to welcome him." (Acts 18:27a) Here the Greek word is PROTREPO, to encourage, exhort.

23. USE HUMOR

Humor is a good starter to witnessing. Laughing with, not at, a person often breaks the ice. A good laugh together creates good fellowship.

24. DEMONSTRATE A SERVANT'S HEART

Jesus is a great example of servanthood. He says, "Not so with you. Instead, whoever wants to become great among you must be your servant, and whoever wants to be first must be your slave--just as the Son of Man did not come to be served, but to serve, and to give his life as ransom for many. (Matthew 20:26-28) Paul reminds us, "Serve wholeheartedly, as if you were serving the Lord, not men." (Ephesians 6:7)

GOOD ROPING !

MANGANA OR BELLYROPE?

The most valuable assets that the Western cowboy possesses are his horse and rope. He takes great pride in developing the skill of utilizing his rope to lasso cows for branding, to "hogtie[2]" a calf in a specified time, and to corral a wild horse. The cowboy's rope, usually 25-60 feet long, is properly prepared through stretching and singeing over a flame in order to "sing" and flow freely. This rope is indispensable. His expertise with it is developed by constant practice. Terminology such as "Mangana," is roping a calf by his forefeet; "throwing a hungry loop," is to catch a wild animal; while "hog-tie" is to bind the two hind and one front legs with a tie rope. Cowboys are embarrassed and ashamed if they throw a "bellyrope" because the lasso is slippery and fails to accomplish the task. A short rope is used for steer roping and branding while the long rope is utilized on wild livestock.

So often the Christian throws a proverbial "bellyrope" thus missing the mark for an effective witness. Throwing "bellyropes" is discouraging for the church-at-large for we throw too many "bellyropes" with slippery lassos. Just as the cowboy's rope is specially prepared for his work, so too we need to prepare ourselves for effective witnessing. Training and practicing are essential—they eliminate slippery lassos.

THROWING THE HOULIHAN

To seasoned cowboys the term "houlihan[3]" has special meaning. This style of roping is utilized primarily for roping horses in a corral. It is an excellent technique when he desires to rope the neck of a specific horse that is standing close to other horses. This roping can be accomplished either on horseback or on foot. Throwing the "houlihan" requires skill, patience, and practice to build the loop, swing the loop, and allow the proper release.

What about your spiritual "houlihans"? As Christians we do not lasso horses, instead we throw the "houlihan" of God's love around a prospect. It takes patience, practice, and skill in our evangelistic lassoing.

THE HACKAMORE

In training a horse you always put on the bridle first. Not so for veteran cowboys. Instead, they use a hackamore which is a loop-shape rawhide nose band which helps the cowboy to communicate his intentions by applying pressure to the jaw and nose. The reins of the hackamore are made of twisted horsehair known as the mecate. A vaquero uses reatas made of braided rawhide for roping cattle. It is more flexible and requires a special technique. Due to its light weight the reata is ideal in windy conditions on the prairies.

God's Law is the rein that keeps sin in check in the world. In evangelism we emphasize Law and Gospel to the prospect.

HOME VISIT

When we visit homes of prospective people we should be cognizant of the surroundings. If there are photos on display it is advantageous to comment about them. Usually your prospect will talk about family, mom and dad may speak about their children. In this way you can gain important insights about family structure and relationships. This is a perfect opportunity to witness. Many times people reveal where they are spiritually hurting and need prayer support. This may give you an opportunity to present your personal testimony emphasizing the great things God has done in your life.

UNCOMFORTABLE

It can be uncomfortable for the church-at-large to realize how important it is to have effective evangelism when they are not witnessing effectively. The congregation struggles in an effort to move ahead in outreach; but then congregations forget. We care and we don't care.

The Great Commission of our Lord is a divine mandate. Evangelism cannot wait; the 911 call of Scripture must be answered. There is an imminent spiritual need of people who do not know Christ as their personal Savior.

COMFORTABLE

Our God wants us to be comfortable in our presentation of relational evangelism. We become comfortable through training, memorizing Scripture, praying, and practicing our skill of articulating the greatest message that the world needs--forgiveness and salvation through Christ.

As we become proficient through training, we are more relaxed and comfortable when we visit with prospects. We become motivated by the love of Christ.

There were numerous times when I took evangelism teams out and in fear some wished, "I hope nobody answers the door when we call." As human beings we all want to be liked and so fear rejection. It is useful to remember that when a person rejects your witness it is not you but the message you are bringing. We need a tougher skin for rejection and more passion for The Great Commission.

TENDERFOOT OR RAWHIDE

The cowboy uses the term "Tenderfoot" to denote an inexperienced wrangler while the term "Rawhide" depicts an experienced cowboy. What appellation describes the average Christian in witnessing? We may be a "Tenderfoot" with no experience at all and believe that the job of reaching the lost is mission impossible. But the mission is possible with Christ. "Jesus looked at them and said, 'With man this is impossible, but with God all things are possible.' " (Matt. 19:26) The Holy Spirit puts the words into our mouths in order to speak the gospel. We are the rawhides in our outreach to the unchurched. Just as it takes practice to be an experienced cowboy, so practice in witnessing is vital.

EXPERIENCED EVANGELISTS

Every experienced cowboy wants to be proficient in roping cattle. This is one of the multifarious tasks of a cowhand. But in order to be proficient in roping he must know how to tie a "honda knot." The spliced eyelet at the end of the rope forms a loop which is called a "honda knot." If he is successful he called it a "hungry loop," and if he missed, it was said "he wasted a loop."

As a cowboy is diligent in learning to tie an effective honda knot, so is the Christian diligent in learning the techniques of witnessing to be proficient in evangelism.

HIT YOUR TARGET!

Both the archer and the marksman aim at their target. The concept is to hit the target's bull's eye every time. It takes years of practice to be proficient in each of these sports and involves hours at the practice range. It is discouraging for a sportsman to miss the target, a sign that more practice is needed.

The unchurched non-Christian carries a target, his soul that does not know Jesus Christ as their personal Savior and Lord. As Christians we articulate the gospel when we witness, sometimes missing the bulls eye, becoming discouraged. Our God encourages us with his words: "Let us not become weary in doing good, for at the proper time we will reap a harvest if we do not give up." (Galatians 6:9)

UTILIZE ROPING

The "Mangan De Cabra" known as the figure 8 is used to catch a calf by the forefeet for a complete job of roping. Sometimes the calf throws off the lasso by wiggling.

In evangelism we sometimes try to wiggle out of our responsibility. There is no fancy roping in witnessing, but there have to be clearly defined lines of accountability.

What kind of a witnessing roper are you? Have you practiced lately?

NOTES

[1] The three Greek words are:

1. EROS The lowest love, erotica 2. PHILEO - Brotherly love 3. AGAPE-God's love toward us. The highest and unconditional love when he sent His son to die for us.

[2] A term to denote the hog-tying of the feet of calves in a quick fashion in order to score a good time at rodeos.

[3] Depicts a loop of lariat tossed with a backhand toss.

CHAPTER SEVEN

GOOD NEWS FROM RANCH HANDS

DOOR-BLOCKERS OR STRETCHER-BEARERS?

When Jesus was at Capernaum, people flocked to see him. (Mark 2:4-12) Jesus was there for a given purpose--namely, to heal the paralytic man who would appear before him. The people were so excited to see Jesus that they became door-blockers to the entrance of the home preventing the stretcher-bearers from entering. Undaunted and with great creativity they made a hole in the thatched roof and lowered the man by ropes to Jesus. What great ingenuity! The stretch-bearers could have given up and rationalized, "We did our job, we took the man from point A to point B. Our job has been completed." But no, they realized that their job was not complete until they brought the sick man into the presence of Christ.

Congregants can either be Gawkers (those who stand idly by and watch), Door blockers (blocking and hindering efforts to bring people to Jesus), Stretcher-bearers (who at all costs bring lost souls to Jesus). Undaunted, sometimes at personal sacrifice, giving freely of time, the Stretcher-bearer will always accomplish the God-given task. A Christian can be a Roof-breaker, also, willing against all odds to take the ultimate risk to tear off the roof in order to bring a person to Christ.

Will you go the second mile to be both a Stretcher-bearer and Roof- breaker, to bring the sin-sick world into the presence of Jesus?

Take a spiritual inventory of your life! Are you a person who stands by and gawks? a Door-blocker? You must make a decision. At times, when our outreach is stymied for one reason or another we tend to lose heart to the point of giving up the whole venture. Let's get creative in bringing people to Jesus in the 21st century!

ROAD BLOCKS TO WITNESSING

What are possible deterrents and roadblocks to witnessing?

+ We are not biblically grounded in the Word.
+ We are fearful.
+ We don't feel equipped.
+ We think it is someone else's job.
+ We do not know the answers to anticipated questions.
+ We do not feel committed.
+ We feel unworthy to talk about Christ.

"Cast all your anxiety on him because he cares for you." (I Peter 5:7) Many Christians approach evangelism with fear. What is the definition of fear?

F-alse
E-xpectations
A-ppear
R-eal

Look to Scripture to assuage fear, "Do not fear the reproach of men nor be terrified by their insults." (Isaiah 51:7b)

BARRIERS TO THE GOSPEL

There are barriers and setbacks to witnessing. Our Lord never said it would be easy. But he did give us the promise of his Word. "As the rain and the snow come down from heaven, and do not return to it without watering the earth and making it bud and flourish, so that it yields seed for the sower and bread for the eater. so is my word that goes out from my mouth: It will not return to me empty, but will accomplish what I desire and achieve the purpose for which I sent it." (Isaiah 51:10-11) What a guarantee from God! Some products try to give a life-time guarantee, but God's guarantee is an eternal and assured guarantee. God's Word is efficacious and his Word never returns to him void, but accomplishes the divine plan that he designed in the lives of individuals.

HAVE YOU LOST YOUR DIRECTION?

Jim, age 9, attended grade school very faithfully achieving perfect attendance. He was bright and always smiling. His teacher was therefore surprised when he missed four days of school. When he returned on the fifth day, she inquired, "Jim, where have you been? We missed you." Jim replied, "Teacher, I lost my steeple." Not understanding this and fearing possible illness she took Jim to the school nurse. When questioned by the nurse he again responded, "I lost my steeple." "Jim, you had better explain, for it just doesn't make sense what you are saying" was her reply. "The steeple of my church always guided me to school so I would never lose my way. During the last 4 days fog clouded my path."

In today's world it is easy for us to "lose our steeple," that is, Jesus Christ as spiritual guide. What about people who have never had a spiritual guide? Parents panic if their children are lost in a crowd—where is our urgency to find those souls lost in the world without a spiritual compass? That compass is Christ. (Luke 15) contains the trilogy of the lost coin, the lost sheep, and the lost sons. Christ's desire is to seek and to save that which was lost. Our mission as Christians is to fulfill Christ's desire.

THE GOSPEL

Decades ago cowboy movies and books were popular. Today they are passé. Yet the American cowboy, or rancher, is very evident in the West. Similarly, today the word evangelism is not used in the true Biblical meaning. Evangelism is biblical for it is derived from the Greek EUANGELION good news, gospel.

Evangelize is what we as Christians do. There is a tendency to substitute words such as "missions," or "outreach" as more relevant; somehow the very word "evangelism" is passé. Let's call it as it as biblical teaching intended---evangelism.

What is your definition of evangelism?

THE GREAT COMMISSION

Jesus, in The Great Commission, gave a mandate to the church "All authority in heaven and on earth has been given to me. Therefore go and make disciples of all nations, baptizing them in the name of the Father and of the Son and of the Holy Ghost, and teaching them to obey everything I have commanded you. And surely I will be with you always, to the very end of the age." (Matthew 28:18-20) The chief theme is MAKE DISCIPLES OF ALL NATIONS. The Lutheran Hour opens every broadcast: "Bringing Christ to the Nations-the Lutheran Hour."

What constitutes a disciple? The Greek word is helpful: MATHETES, a learner, one who follows.

Many congregations have a Pastor of Discipleship whose role is to nurture members of the congregation in all aspects of Bible study. The mandate that Christ gives to the church is not a suggestion nor is it an item to place on hold for the next voters' meeting. It is, and should be, marching orders for the church. Do you personally take this mandate seriously? The twelve disciples of Jesus took this mandate so seriously that all except John suffered martyrdom for the sake of the gospel. They spread the gospel to the far corners of the known world of their day.

WITNESS BY CONVICTION

Any salesman will say that personal contacts are best for sales. This is also true with regard to evangelism. Contact must be personal, relational, heart-to-heart in reaching out to the unchurched. The ideal is to build relationships over a period of time. There are situations which arise when we can witness "in passing," such as when traveling. We may see that person this side of eternity in heaven. Whatever the situation, it is important to not lose sight of the gospel. It is easy to concentrate on building the relationship because it is easier than articulating the gospel message. Witness should demonstrate not only our love and concern for the person to whom we are witnessing but also our love for Christ.

We can learn from the Christmas angels who announced the birth of Christ to the lowly shepherds on the first Christmas Eve "Do not be afraid, I bring you good news of great joy that will be for all people. Today in the town of David a Savior has been born to you; he is Christ the Lord." (Luke 2:10-11) What is the content of that message? There is joy in the Gospel message! It needs no "watering down!" Speak clearly of your joy in Jesus Christ as your personal Savior from sin..

DIG IN YOUR SPURS!

The letter to the Hebrews states, "And let us consider how we may spur[1] one another on toward love and good deeds." (Hebrews 10:24) The spurs of a cowboy are designed to incite the horse to move forward. The gospel spurs Christians to be actively involved in evangelism. Reliance on the power of the Holy Spirit is paramount to incite, motivate, and stir us up for more action as we spread the Good News of salvation. Dig in your spurs! Move ahead with an evangelism program in your church!

MARS HILL

When we read our newspapers and view the news on TV most of the information is bad news. It has been said by newspaper editors that bad news sells better than good news. People want to know about scams, scandals, or malfeasance by a politician. The gospel is always good news. It is the news that Christ died for our sins to perfect our salvation.

Have you realized the blessings of this good news? When Paul was at the synagogue in Athens the Stoics and Epicurean philosophers tried to dispute what Paul was preaching. "They said this because Paul was preaching the good news about Jesus and the resurrection." (Acts 17:18) When he was at the Areopagus on Mars Hill he preached to the intelligentsia of his day, "For as I walked around and observed your objects of worship, I even found an altar with this inscription: TO AN UNKNOWN GOD. Now what you worship as something unknown I am going to proclaim to you." (Acts 17:23) On two separate tours in the footsteps of St. Paul, I climbed to the top of Mars Hill to see exactly where Paul preached his powerful message. There is a panoramic view of the surrounding area from this vantage point. When Paul was in Antioch in Syria the Scriptures declare: "They preached the good news in that city and won a large number of disciples." (Acts 14:21)

SOME GOOD NEWS

Bad news such as scandal, fraud and crime sell newspapers. Good news is relegated to the back pages of newspapers and to the end of news broadcasts.

Christians must boldly exclaim, "Extra! Extra! Read all about it! Jesus Christ died for your sins and rose victorious on the first Easter morning to assure your salvation!" The Holy Spirit creates faith to claim Jesus as our personal Savior.

THE CHURCH THAT FAILS TO EVANGELIZE WILL FOSSILIZE!

THE SUNDAY ASSEMBLY MOVEMENT

People stay away from worship services for a variety of reasons. Most of the excuses in all generations seem plausible. But are they? About two years ago a group was founded in England called The Sunday Assembly Movement. Initiated by London comedians Sanderson Jones and Pippa Evans, it is now spreading at a great rate across the United States. What is this movement? Their meetings consist of speeches, dancing, poetry and refreshments. Some people think that the assembly reaches individuals that the church hasn't reached. People are basically religious. The Assembly is an attempt to fill the emptiness in their lives. In reality, it is a menacing humanistic group that tries to undermine Christianity.

What a challenge to the church! We have to work with ever more diligence to articulate the gospel of Jesus Christ. Time is passing! People's emptiness must be filled with the message of the forgiveness of sins through Christ. Will you stand up and meet this challenge? Paul's great words amonish us, "In the presence of God and of Christ Jesus, who will judge the living and the dead, and in view of his appearing and his kingdom, I give you this charge: Preach the Word; be prepared in season and out of season; correct, rebuke and encourage--with great patience and careful instruction. For the time will come when men will not put up with sound doctrine. Instead, to suit their own desires, they will gather around them a great number of teachers to say what their itching ears want to hear. They will turn their ears away from the truth and turn aside to myths. But you, keep your head in all situations, endure hardship, do the work of an evangelist, discharge all the duties of your ministry." (2 Timothy 4:1-5)

THE CHURCH'S PROCLAMATION

In Luke 4:18, 19 when Jesus returned to his hometown of Nazareth and went into the synagogue he quoted the prophet Isaiah, "The Spirit of the Lord is on me, because he has anointed me to preach good news to the poor. He has sent me to proclaim freedom for the prisoners and recovery of sight for the blind, to release the oppressed, to proclaim the year of the Lord's favor." (Isaiah 61:1-2.) What is the proclamation[2] of the church? Simply stated, mankind is reconciled to God through Christ. A balanced sermon comprises both Law and Gospel. If there is only Law, people despair with no hope. If only Gospel, people may become proud and self-righteous. An experienced Pastor has been trained to preach a balance of Law and Gospel in his weekly sermons to articulate the "good news" in his message of evangelism. "For Christ died for our sins once for all,[3] the righteous for the unrighteous, to bring you to God. He was put to death in the body but made alive by the Spirit." (I Peter 3:18) It took the sinless Son of God to pay the penalty for our sins to the heavenly Father, truly the just for the unjust. "In him we have redemption through his blood, the forgiveness of sins, in accordance with the riches of God's grace." (Ephesians 1:7)

THE FUTURE FOR BIOPRINTING

Scientists at Wake Forest University in Winston-Salem, North Carolina, are making great advances in bio-printing--the process that replicates human organs using specialized 3-D printers The first organ produced was a human ear. This specialized 3-D printer utilizes syringes to produce numerous layers of matter to produce a three-dimensional item. The end product is an object that is alive. This special machine has 6 syringes in a row. One syringe contains a biocompatible plastic that forms a human body part; the other syringes are filled with a substance of human cells to promote the growth of the specified organ. The printed cells of the scaffold are inserted into an incubator for multiplication.

This is revolutionary! Just think, in a few years when you need an organ or other body part you can say to your doctor, "Hey, Doc, I need a new body part!" Doctors and scientists are still trying to produce a functional heart and kidney. We wish them great success. This process is a great advancement in medical science.

What does this have to do with evangelism? Scientists are still struggling to produce a functional heart through bio-printing and may someday succeed. Meanwhile, in 2016, the heart is the subject of our investigation. Scriptures have a lot to say about the heart. Searching the Bible, there are countless references to the heart in both the Old Testament and the New Testament, Jesus says, "Out of the heart comes evil thoughts, murder, adultery, sexual immorality, theft, false testimony, slander." (Matthew 15:19) "I will give you a new heart and put a new spirit in you; I will remove from your heart of stone and give you a heart of flesh." (Ezekiel 36:26)

A TRANSFORMATION

The "Good News" of the gospel transforms us into new people in Christ. Through Christ's precious blood we are transformed sinners, that is, we are both saints and sinners. We sin daily but daily receive the forgiveness of all of our sins through Christ. Transformed by Christ from the old life to the new, we are motivated by the Holy Spirit to speak the message of salvation to everyone.

SAINTS

Suzie, age 10, loved Sunday School even more than day school. She received perfect attendance medals every year. One Sunday, when her Sunday School class was held in the church which had beautiful stained-glass windows, the teacher was explaining the definition of a saint, "Class, a saint is a sinner who believes in Christ as their Savior." Trying to get a response from the other pupils she noticed Suzie daydreaming and asked her, "Suzie, what is your definition of a saint?" Suzie contemplated for a few moments and replied; "Saints are people who let the light shine through." Suzie had it right, she would make a great evangelist. Prospects have to see Christ not only from the Word but also through us. Sometimes we stand in the shadows, failing to reflect the light to the world.

COWBOY BOOTS

The American cowboy takes great pride in owning comfortable boots. Leisure. or "dress" boots especially, are made by skillful craftsmen and styled by famous designers such as Beck, Buffalo Run, Tony Lama. Boots may be customized for a perfect fit. People who wear boots praise them for their long-wear and comfort. Comfort and style are expensive, but boots usually last a long time making them a worthwhile investment.

Feet are not particularly attractive. As human beings we do everything possible to make them look good using varieties of style and color. In God's sight, feet are beautiful because they are useful, "How beautiful on the mountains are the feet of those who bring good news, who proclaim peace, who bring good tidings, who proclaim salvation, who say to Zion, "Your God reigns" (Isaiah 52:7)

Sometimes a clothing label says "one size fits all" and sometimes that is true." But when it comes to evangelism one size does NOT fit all. Consideration of different individuals and personalities is the relational, one-on-one approach to evangelism. It is by far the most effective. Just as cowboy boots are customized to fit one person, we too in evangelism have to customize our approach in witnessing. How comfortable are your evangelism boots? Are they comfortable enough to have the real zeal to be comfortable in everyday situations using the one-to-one approach to a prospect?

SOLES FOR SOULS

A young missionary was sent to Africa to establish an indigenous mission church. When he left the United States he was very mission-minded but upon arriving at the airport in Africa he was disillusioned. He said, "None of these people have shoes. I can't serve these savages." He returned to the U.S. Years later another missionary was sent to the same area of Africa. When he arrived, he said "These people do not have shoes. What a mission outreach to not only provide soles for their feet but the gospel for their souls." It was a matter of perspective.

At times there is frustration in evangelism and it is quite easy to lose perspective and become disillusioned as did the first missionary. The Pastor is the chief motivator in keeping the congregation focused on The Great Commission and the joy that success brings to the Christian.

THE BRAKEMAN'S LANTERN

The brakeman is an integral position of a well-maintained train. The brakeman's duties include seeing that all cars are attached properly, that the track is clear, that he is able to alert of impending dangers not only his train but other trains along the track.

A brakeman was once called to testify at a trial when one freight train accidentally crashed into a passenger train causing 80 deaths. The defense attorney interrogated the brakeman at the trial. He posed such questions as: "Did you try to warn the other train of the impending danger?" "Yes," was the reply. "Did you wave your special lantern?" "Yes," was the answer again. The prosecuting attorney was skeptical of the brakeman's answers. The prosecution asked one question, "Was your lantern functioning and did it shed light?" "No," "was the reply. The brakeman was indicted for failure to alert the other train.

We as Christians often mirror the brakeman's behavior in that we go through the motions--we wave the lantern, we try to warn the unrepentant and we fail miserably. Why? We do not have our spiritual lights on and so cannot point others to Jesus Christ as the light of the world. Trains have accidents. Train cars are derailed and explosions occur along the rail lines. Many people are making a train wreck of their lives because they do not know that Jesus Christ is their Savior.

THE ENGINE LIGHT

On several occasions I have experienced the engine light suddenly blinking on the dashboard of my vehicle. Mechanics tell us that this light indicates minor or serious malfunction. In any case, it should be repaired. It could be that the air pollution converter needs changing, a procedure absolutely necessary after so many miles of driving. If not attended, serious engine damage can result. It is best to have the engine light checked.

Sometimes God sends a warning light into our lives to alert us to our spiritual condition. When we minimize or ignore this light, spiritual damage to our souls can result.

A CREATIVE WAY OF COMMUNICATION

Prisons have been with us in every century. In the 1500's there was great security and surveillance of prisoners. No one was able to smuggle contraband or messages to the prisoners from the outside community. However, messages were smuggled using chicken eggs! How was this done? The plan was simple, yet creative. Writing a message in ink on the outside shell, the smuggler would allow the ink to dry for 20 minutes, then boil the egg in water and alum for 5 minutes. The message on the egg shell disappeared, and reappeared when the prisoner removed the eggshell. The message got through in spite of every obstacle.

Great tenacity of purpose and creativity are needed to have a viable communication plan for evangelism. It is well to gather all the talent available in a congregation to maximize the creative process. Without using eggshells, there are many ways to effectively spread the gospel message that God loves everyone. Using today's social media, for example, thousands of people can know instantly that Jesus Christ died to set us free from sin, death, and the power of the devil. We are washed in the blood of the Lamb.

A CATALYST FOR THE GOSPEL

Augustine said: "Preach the Word by your life and even use the words of the gospel." Our lives are open books to the world! A catalyst in chemistry is an item that effects a change but itself is not changed. This must be true for our effective witness of the gospel. Without allowing the world to change us, we must be catalysts in a world that is apathetic to the message of the Word of God. By the life we live, we reflect that God is our owner.

If your great goal in life is to be rich at any cost and use power to control people, then you belong to the world. But if you look to Christ, and focus solely on him in everything that you do and say, then your owner is Christ. In your heart, you carry his brand--the cross.

As Christians we have to search our hearts to see if we have added to the apathy of non-Christians by our lack of action in evangelism.

A WHISPER

The Lord confronted Elijah, "the Prophet of Fire." He told the prophet to watch as the Lord will pass by. "Then a great and powerful wind tore the mountains apart and shattered the rocks before the Lord, but the Lord was not in the wind. After the wind there was an earthquake, but the Lord was not in the earthquake. After the earthquake came a fire, but the Lord was not in the fire. And after the fire came a gentle whisper." (I Kings 19:11b-12)

This is the way our everyday life may be. We think that God speaks in humdrum ways. Here it is a whisper. God, through his Holy Spirit, whispers in our ears to be bold proclaimers of the gospel. Elijah had to fight great odds in his day. There may be times when we, too, have spiritual battles to fight for the sake of the gospel.

The Christian develops ease with practice. The result is a bold proclamation of faith that might just move your prospect. Training pays off in the corporate world, so it can in the spiritual world. There will not be a ledger showing profit or loss but God's own ledger in heaven that a soul was won for Christ. It would be deleterious not to practice our witnessing. You may have taken evangelism training in the past without good results. Did you actually practice witnessing?

The salient question is, "Have you put that training into action and gleaned the experience and joy of witnessing?" It is important to articulate the grace of God in our lives.

Here is a simple way to remember the biblical definition of grace:

G-od's
R-iches
A-t
C-hrist's
E-xpense

FAITH

How often have you heard someone say, "You just have to have faith." What do they mean? Faith in a tree? Faith in a person? Faith in science? Faith must have an object. For Christians that object is Christ, faith in the merits of Jesus Christ for our eternal salvation.

"Now faith is being sure of what we hope for and certain of what we do not see." (Hebrews 11:1) Hebrews chapter 11 is the great hero chapter that delineates all the great saints of God who lived by faith. The chapter begins "By faith . . ." The Greek word PISTOS means faith and is used in the Bible in two ways. In the passive voice, faithful in reference to God and in the active voice meaning believing, trusting, relying.

THE BIG COVER UP

A "cover up" in society, whether in government or industry, signifies an effort to hide something. Think of medicines on the market. Advertising would have us believe that a certain medicine will heal. Pharmaceutical companies often wait until a class action suit is filed before they report the deleterious effect of a drug. Thus, the Food and Drug Administration warns the public or recalls a drug. Sometimes the recall comes too late to save a patient. Another way to cover up is to stretch the truth by stating lie upon lie--covering up one falsehood with another.

Do you realize there is a big cover up in the Scriptures? It doesn't mean something negative, but in this case something very positive. "Blessed is he whose transgressions are forgiven, whose sins are covered." (Psalm 32:1) Through Christ we have been reconciled to God. We stand before God through Christ in an AT-ONE-MENT relationship. "In him we have redemption through his blood, the forgiveness of sins, in accordance with the riches of God's grace." (Ephesians. 1:7)

CHRIST IS OUR RIGHTEOUSNESS

Dr. Martin Luther, great Reformer of the Lutheran Reformation, has written many books and treatises that he translated from the Latin Vulgate into everyday German for his people. The printing press, invented by Gutenberg, was instrumental in spreading the pure gospel to all of Germany. It was Luther's initial intention to purge the false doctrine of the Papacy of his time. When that was not possible, he made a complete break from the Roman Church. It was his "Tower Experience" where he discovered the Scriptural verse "The righteous shall live by faith" (Romans 1:17b) that gave great momentum to the Lutheran reformation. Luther emphasized that Christ, by his vicarious atonement, satisfied the justice of God the Father and reconciled the world to God. Man had to be reconciled to God. The only way was by the crucifixion and resurrection of Jesus Christ. "That God was reconciling the world to himself in Christ, not counting men's sins against them. And he committed to us the message of reconciliation."[4] (2 Corinthians 5:19) The "suffering servant" motif is utilized in Scripture by Isaiah in Chapter 53. This chapter is read in most churches during Lent and especially on Good Friday. Luther amplifies this verse in his commentary to a friend: "Learn to know Christ and him crucified. Learn to sing to him and say, 'Lord Jesus, you are my righteousness, I am your sin. You have taken upon yourself what is mine and given me what is yours. You became what you were not, so that I might become what I was not.[5] '"

CONFORMITY-NO!

Our archenemy Satan employs the ways of conformity in order to keep our focus off of Christ and on things of this world. Jell-O molds have been used by housewives for many years. Jell-O and pudding are poured into plastic molds. When it "jells" a delicious dessert is the result.

So it is with the distractions of the world--they are there to press us into a conforming mold--molds of misconduct, sin, unethical living and rebellion against God. There are civil laws of our country that every Christian as a good citizen obeys. Paul reminds us, "Do not conform[6] any longer to the pattern of this world, but be transformed[7] by the renewing of your mind." (Romans 12:2) Changed attitudes, changed minds, changed desires, and changed hearts, God wants us to stand out among the crowd and to take a stand for Christ our Lord!

THE REVITALIZATION MODE

Evangelism is a revitalization mode for every congregation. Churches train their members for outreach in their communities. We build a relational mode of evangelism through neighborhood events. Daily we should pray "O Lord, today, may your Holy Spirit guide me to speak the Word of reconciliation to some person." The child of God is living in a state of grace. We waver, sin, stumble, and falter along life's pilgrimage, but God's Holy Spirit calls us back to the straight path. Transfiguration Sunday is an important day in liturgical churches. Jesus took his Inner Circle of Disciples (Peter, James, and John) to Mt. Hermon and he was transfigured before them. It was a complete metamorphosis. Moses, representing the Law appeared on one side and Elijah, representing the Prophets appeared on the other. "When they looked up, they saw no one except Jesus." (Matthew 17:8) We must see Jesus and Jesus only in our daily lives as he comes to us in Word and Sacrament. In all of your evangelism effort, are you seeing Jesus, and Jesus only?

PASS THE BATON

Relay teams train arduously. To win a relay race their timing must be perfect when they "pass the baton." Even on professional teams occasionally a runner drops the baton thus losing the team's place in the outcome of the relay race. Christians are runners for the gospel of Jesus Christ and are on a spiritual relay team carrying, not a baton, but the "good news" of Jesus Christ. Don't drop your baton! Don't hold on to the baton of the gospel, but pass it on!

SABOTAGE

During all wars there have been saboteurs on both sides who were specially trained to cripple the enemy. Sabotage is alive even today. Its methods have grown more sophisticated over time; for example, using computers, hackers steal government secrets and documents.

Satan the Slanderer, is active in the church and doesn't want a congregation to have an evangelism program. Pastor and people can think of a dozen reasons for not doing outreach and Satan helps them along through gossip, mistrust, innuendo and other inventive ways, thus sabotaging an evangelism program.

CHANGE YOUR NAME!

Alexander the Great is renowned in ancient history as a military genius. He conquered many empires during his short span of life. He lamented, "There are no more worlds to conquer." One time a soldier of Alexander's army was brought before the general on an AWOL charge. Alexander interrogated him thoroughly in order to determine the cause of the soldier's fear and timidity in battle. "Man, what is your name?" asked Alexander the Great. The recruit mumbled the words, almost inaudibly, "Alexander, Sir." The great general scolded the soldier and said, "Change your life or change your name!" How true that is for Christians. Are we living up to the name "Christian?" What are you projecting to the world? Is it the love and concern for souls?

NOTES

1 The Greek word is PAROXUSMON, meaning "provoke, how to spur." Provoke means to excite for a worthy purpose. The R.S.V. states, "to stir up one another in love and good works."

2 The Greek KERUZAI, meaning "to be a herald, proclaim." KERUGMA means "message, preaching."

3 HAPAX translates "once for all," here and in Jude 3. EPAPAX is stronger than HAPAX as noted in Romans 6:10 and Hebrews 7:27.

4 Here, KATALLASSON means "reconciling." KATALLASSO, 'to reconcile." Originally it meant the exchange of money. Here it is a change from enemy to friendship. Paul never used the word DIALLASSO meaning a "mutual concession after mutual hostility."

5 Packer, James. *Your Father Loves You* Harold Shaw Publishers, 1986.

6 The Greek is SUSCHEMATIZESTHE "be not conformed." Romans 12:2 contrasts being outwardly "conformed" to the things of this world with being transformed inwardly by the Holy Spirit.

7 The Greek is METAMORPHOUSTHE "be transformed."

CHAPTER EIGHT

DON'T FOLLOW THE HERD: INNOVATIVE TECHNIQUES

HERD MENTALITY

One of the dangers on the trail is stampedes. Cattle are easily "spooked." In most herds a prominent steer assumes the lead to guide the herd. The cowboy allows this steer to be the guide throughout the drive. Cowboys always use preventative measures in order to ameliorate an inevitable stampede. When herds stampede there is a tendency for the herd to replicate that response.

What preventative measures do congregations use when the flock is in danger of being "spooked" (fear of witnessing) or to stop a stampede (people leaving)? Regardless of denomination there is still "herd mentality" with regard to the vision.

A psychologist intensely researched "follow the crowd psychology (herd mentality)." He noticed people jump on the proverbial band wagon following the particular behavior of a crowd. They assumed the majority were right. He thought to himself "I am a well trained psychologist- this will never happen to me." Well, it did one day when he joined a picket line of strikers without evaluating the reason for their actions. He followed the crowd. This is especially true in congregations wherein a small faction believes they have the right answer in every situation and also the ability to convince other people to follow them.

We tend to follow the way of the world without thinking about vision, goals or objectives. Do you and your congregation have a vision? What are your short-term and long-term goals? Do you have clear-cut objectives for reaching those goals?

THE TRAIL BOSS

A cattle "drive" is only one-half of the story. Only on the first day is the herd of cattle driven. This is so that they will be more submissive for the long trail ahead. Actually, cowboys use "trailing" as the more correct term. The "trail boss" is the chief cowboy who rides ahead of the herd to scout out new pastures and to find camping each night. He must also envision possible dangers and take preventative measures to protect the herd.

The Pastor of a congregation is similar to a trail boss for he is the visionary who sets the tone of the congregation and takes the lead in evangelism. If the pastor fails in this, evangelism will suffer. Very often pastors say, "This is MY vision for MY congregation." Actually, that statement is misleading, for the congregation does not belong to him. He is merely the shepherd.

It is imperative that the Pastor and congregation develop an evangelism plan together. If these plans differ, the following situations may arise: People become disgruntled and respond by leaving the congregation altogether. Or, if, after a previous long pastorate, the congregation fails to engage an Interim Pastor and the new Pastor makes changes too quickly, disaster may follow. People can become confused about the vision. A new Pastor may not have the same vision as his new congregation. Vox populi is vital. It may take several sessions (not just one, or one day) for the Pastor and congregation to communicate an evangelism vision that each understands and agrees upon.

Have you ever stood in line for hours or even camped out for days in order to buy an expensive electronic component? By standing in line or camping overnight you try to convince yourself that the item is "such a good buy" that standing in line is worth the wait. We may even bolster our action by thinking "Everyone else is standing in line, it has to be valuable, and I have to own it."

"Social proof" denotes people purchasing items that are either over-priced or limited in quantity. This was true when Cabbage Patch dolls were the "must-have" item for girls. Some parents were so determined to buy the doll for their child that physical battles in stores were not uncommon. This was a classic example of "herd mentality."

WE ARE LARGE ENOUGH

Many large congregations assume that because they are large (3,000+) there is no need to reach out to their community. They lull themselves to sleep with the notion that transfers in from other churches are the only criteria for growth. They say, "We just can't accommodate more members." "Good for you (to a degree) and for the moment." I am glad that you are presently growing by leaps and bounds. But what will your congregation look like 20 or 30 years from now? Do you have an outreach program? Do you have a Board of Evangelism? I hope so. I have seen so many congregations of all denominations close their doors and actually fossilize due to the lack of evangelism in their immediate area.

FLEXIBLE

Cowboys refer to a specially trained horse as a "peg horse" that possesses the ability to run full speed ahead, change direction, and stop quickly. Christians, in evangelism, must learn to be that flexible in their presentations of the gospel message. When things are going well we do not like to change: indeed, we fear change. However, we are sometimes compelled to change by factors beyond our control. Above all, be flexible in outreach.

STRAYS

In every herd of cattle there are cows that have a proclivity to stray from the herd. The diligent cowboy utilizes every skill he has to corral these strays and bring them back. There are also "strays" in the church--people straying from the Scriptures and from worship. A passion for souls and the gospel message are needed to bring the strays back. The big question is, "What is your relationship to Jesus Christ?" Pay particular attention to the answer as it will be your guide to returning that lost soul to Christ.

SETTLER

How often we hear from a family who have moved into a new home and lived there for several months, "We are now settled in our home." To the family this means that familiar things are around them and they are comfortable. When we refer to the foundation or the pavement of a house we say that it has it has "settled," a word that has a negative connotation.

Without doubt, church members are settled in their ways. Usually they do not want to try something new. It can be easier (requiring less effort) to simply watch another church try something new and then copy them. Following the status quo lets you sit back in the comfortable rocking chair of Christianity. "We never did it that way before," meaning, "We will not change, we won't try something new."

PIONEER

We marvel at the initiative, fortitude, and determined spirit of the first pioneers who forged ahead in exploring this country and found new areas of endeavor. They endured harsh climate, disease, hostile Indians, and disillusionment. But with a pioneering spirit they accomplished their goal while paving the way for others to follow. We need less "settlers," and more pioneers in the church to accomplish what our Lord wants us to do. The pioneer takes risks, tries new methods, and launches ahead in church work. We need a group of dedicated men and women who possess a pioneering spirit to forge ahead in new challenges in evangelism!

DIFFERENT VIEWS OF EVANGELISM

People of the world have various views of evangelism. This is true even within the church.

Let us look at some of the negative and positive views of evangelism.

NEGATIVE PERSPECTIVES	POSITIVE PERSPECTIVES
1) TV preachers	1) Loving
2) Radio evangelists	2) Caring
3) Pushy people, superior attitude	3) Non-judgmental
4) Too busy, not my role	4) Accepts a person where they are
5) My church is big enough	5) Witness in daily situations
6) I am satisfied with my faith	6) Together makes an impact
7) Will not share my beliefs	7) Get excited about faith
8) We-have-done-it-before	8) Searches out biblical truths
9) Church terms unfamiliar to the unchurched	9) Positive attitude

There are times Christians follow the least path of resistance, or the Pastor works feverishly to apply oil to the squeaky wheel.

LIPIZZANER

Vienna, Austria is noted for two items, namely Vienna concerts and the Lipizzaner horses. The horses received their nomenclature from a stud farm located in Lipica, Slovenia. These horses are bred, trained, and shown in great horse shows in Vienna. The colts run rampant through the pastures and during that time learn to recognize a certain stallion as the head of the herd. He has a bell around his neck and when it rings the other colts follow him. Truly this is a positive example of following the herd.

But in evangelism the Lord doesn't want us to follow the herd, but to follow his lead in fulfilling the The Great Commission he has given as a divine mandate to his church.

COME RAIN OR COME SHINE

Bobby was a member of a Little League baseball team in his community. He listened to every word from his coach, attended all of the practices and wanted to be a professional baseball player when he reached adulthood. The coach would always remind the team "Teamwork and practice are vital for a winning team. I want you out on the diamond come rain or come shine." Within a few weeks a threatening rainstorm was predicted for the area. As he was returning from grocery shopping, the coach, felt the rain. He hurried to the diamond to see if any players were present in spite of the impending rain storm. But there was one lonely figure on the field, and it was Bobby. The coach said "Bobby, what are you doing here? Practice is canceled." Bobby replied "Coach you said you wanted the team to practice come rain or come shine, I am here." We need more Bobbys in the church who are willing to attend meetings, assume the responsibilities of leadership, and serve.

"Step-up-to-the-plate" to hit a home run for Christ!

(PASTOR) + (CONGREGATION) + (TRAINING) = SUCCESS
(COACH) + (TEAM) + (PRACTICE) = SUCCESS

PRAYER WALK

Many congregations have utilized Prayer Walks as a form of outreach in their community. Basically, a group of mission-minded people gather at a team member's home to prayer walk that member's neighborhood. Maps and area assignments are given and teams of two go out-- one person on each side of the block. They ring the door bell ask the resident "We are from _____ Church and doing a Prayer Walk in your neighborhood. Is there a special prayer you would like us to say for you or your family" If yes, PRAY ON THE SPOT FOR THEIR PRAYER NEEDS!. It is good to give them a 4x6 card listing your church or mission and where they may contact you for further spiritual aid. This procedure allows the person to take charge and you do not threaten their privacy by asking for their name, address, and phone number. If "No!, go on to the next house. Coordinate with all involved on the teams to set a definite time (e.g., 2-3 hours) for the Prayer Walk.

At the end, gather at home base to recap experiences. Recap can prove to be both enlightening and edifying. This is another method where callers can learn to pray *ex corde*. At times the resident may reply, "I have everything covered" or "I am doing great." Suggest that you will pray for their continued health and success from the Lord. Community Prayer Walks and Neighborhood Canvasses are passé and both have proven to be ineffective in reaching the unchurched.

BRAIN- STORMING

Brain-storming is not new and has been proven an effective tool to motivate members allowing them to think freely about their congregation and the programs they desire. Many times I would call a Sunday supper meeting and place large placards along the walls. I asked members to call out their dreams, plans, prayers, and aspirations now and for the future. No matter if the item seemed to be frivolous, it was jotted down on the placard. When the placards were completely filled I asked the people to think over all the suggestions. We prayed about these items. The governing board then utilized these ideas to formulate a vision and a vision statement. This exercise focused the church's effort to determine the whys and wherefores of fulfilling that vision in the vineyard where the Lord placed them.

THE BATTLE PLAN

The Battle of Poltava, Russia probably means nothing to Americans. But to Peter the Great of Russia and King Charles of Sweden it was a decisive battle. King Charles had been wounded in a previous battle where he sustained an injury to his foot and had to be carried in a stretcher to the battlefield. On June 27, 1709, Charles formulated a battle plan in order to defeat the Russians. Charles, physically unable to command his army, chose two outstanding officers to lead his army. Rehnskjold would serve as the general of the cavalry and Lewenhaupt would be the general of the infantry. King Charles and Rehnskjold devised a unique battle plan that included speed, surprise, and fast movement past the redoubts. Because Rehnskjold disliked Lewenhaupt, he only revealed a piecemeal plan to each battalion, majors, and quartermasters, failing to communicate the complete battle plan to Lewenhaupt. The final result--the Swedish army was defeated at Poltava by Peter the Great due to lack of communication.

What is the battle plan in the church? Is it an all-encompassing plan that is known by everyone from the janitor to the elders? Or is it the vision of only the Senior Pastor? Is it an obfuscated plan given out piecemeal where no one knows the total plan? This is like belonging to a secret organization. Sometimes members of churches feel this way when they do not participate in formulating the vision. The following are ways to have everyone "on board" with the vision: 1) If a Pastor is new in a parish he should not make changes for one year. 2) Visit members in their homes in order to know them. 3) Procure input from the TOTAL congregation, not from a chosen few. 4) Have sectional brain-storming sessions. 5) Formulate reachable short-term and long-term goals. 6) Set up wall placards at each brainstorm meeting to write down ideas no matter how far-fetched they may seem at the time. This exercise gives everyone an equal opportunity to contribute and creates "buy-in."

OUR RAINBOW OF VISION

During my seven Intentional Interims where I served congregations in California and Arizona, I developed a chart termed "OUR RAINBOW OF VISION" that depicted a colorful rainbow. Members completed 3x5 cards listing their dreams, challenges, prayers, and expectations they had for their congregation during the interim, before a new pastor was called. Then, during the interim, members worked together to accomplish their goals whether short- or long-term. The short-term goals were for the interim and the long-term goals were aspirations for the new pastor's consideration.

The format is based in Scriptures, "Where there is no vision, the people perish." (Proverbs 29:18) Every congregation should be challenged by a clear-cut vision with realistic, attainable, God-pleasing goals. Congregants become very creative in designing OUR RAINBOW OF VISION. They all have two items in common: The title Our Rainbow of Vision and placement of colored ribbons flowing from the rainbow to a card on which the goal is listed. This format could be effective in every congregation that has a clear-cut vision and wants the vision posted conspicuously in the church proper. Members thus graphically and often view the challenges and aspirations of their congregation. When the task has been fulfilled, the card is removed from the rainbow. Members are also encouraged to add new cards (goals) as they desire; for example, new carpet in the sanctuary, new addition, increase in Sunday School attendance, a more effective evangelism program.

"OUR RAINBOW OF VISION"

"Where there is no vision, the people perish." (Proverbs 29:18)

A LITANY FOR VISION

Pastor: Lord, God, we come before Your presence to seek Your will.

People: Guide us, direct us, by Your gracious will.

Pastor: May we come before Your presence with the dreams, expectations, and challenges of our parish.

People: Guide us, direct us, by Your gracious will.

Pastor: "Lengthen your cords, strengthen your stakes."

People: Guide us, direct us, by Your gracious will.

Pastor: As a congregation, let us see the challenges that await us in the future.

People: Guide us, direct us, by Your gracious will.

Pastor: Forgive us when we have been remiss to meet the challenges.

People: Guide us, direct us, by Your gracious will.

Pastor: Utilize the resources at our disposal and the willing hands of Your people.

People: Guide us, direct us, by Your gracious will.

Pastor: May we heed the Scriptures, "There are different kinds of gifts, but the same Spirit" and use our spiritual gifts for Your kingdom.

People: Guide us, direct us, by Your gracious will.

Pastor: Bless our Committee for their diligent work.

People: Guide us, direct us, by Your gracious will.

Members will be given the opportunity to write down on 3 x 5 cards their dream, challenges, prayers, and expectations in "Our Rainbow of Vision." The cards will be collected by the ushers and brought to the altar. During the week, they shall be attached to the multi-colored ribbons for everyone to view.

DEDICATION:

Lord, God, heavenly Father, we bring before You our requests of dreams, challenges, prayers, and expectations as we look forward to the future of this congregation. We ask this in Jesus' name. Amen.

CHAPTER NINE

THE CHUCK-WAGON: A DIAGNOSIS FOR TREATMENT

THE COWBOY'S CHUCK-WAGON

The chuck wagon was the commissary on the trail. It contained everything--food, pots, cooking utensils, cow-chips for the fires, bedrolls and clothes for each cowboy. They ate well while on the trail. Staples included Mexican beans, sourdough bread and meat. Occasionally there was a "surprise"--when the cook delighted them with bacon, oysters, and stew. On larger trail drives the cook might have a second wagon which was called the "trail wagon." At the end of a hard day driving cattle cowboys enjoyed KOINONIA (fellowship) around the campfire as they related their experiences of the day. When food was ready, "Cookie" shouted out, "COME, AND GET IT!"

SPIRITUAL FOOD OF THE CHURCH

The church, as a beacon shining in the impenetrable darkness of the world, feebly says, "COME AND GET IT!" Congregations rationalize and say to themselves "We are here, the doors are open, people should flock to us." This does not happen. What may have been effective in years past is no longer effective today. Jesus says "to make disciples." The church has to reach out to the community with the gospel. The church can no longer be a" "poor man's country club," but must be a dynamo with the message. "I am not ashamed of the gospel, because it is the power of God for the salvation of everyone who believes" (Romans 1:16) The Greek word is DYNAMIS (power.) The Word has that dynamic power to change the hearts of mankind. The Bible offers spiritual food that never spoils, is never out-of-date and is as vibrant as ever.

PRECIOUS LIVING WATER

The cowboy, in selecting a ranch, would seek out land near water in order to claim the water rights. When Jesus came through Samaria he spoke to the woman at Jacob's Well in Sychar. She questioned Jesus's request for water from the well because Jews and Samaritans were enemies. Jesus answered her, "Everyone who drinks this water will be thirsty again, but whoever drinks the water I give him will never thirst. Indeed, the water I give him will become in him a spring of water, welling up to eternal life."(John 4: 13-14)

In desert areas of our country water is scarce and has to be utilized judiciously. Good stewards of the land know this. It is possible to live a long period of time without food, but only a short time without water. The rule of thumb in desert communities is--NEVER GO HIKING ALONE. ALWAYS HAVE AT LEAST ANOTHER HIKER WITH YOU. TAKE PLENTY OF WATER, CELL PHONE, COMPASS, A MAP, AND NOTIFY LOVED ONES WHERE YOU ARE HIKING.

THE ONLY THIRST QUENCHER

Beverages such as Gatorade, Coca-Cola, and Lemonade claim to quench our thirst. But do they? Truly there is only one real thirst-quencher and that is aqua mineral-WATER. The prophet says "Come, all you who are thirsty, come to the waters, and you who have no money, come, buy, and eat! Come buy wine and milk without money and without cost. Why spend money on what is not bread, and your labor on what does not satisfy? Listen, listen to me, and eat what is good, and your soul will delight in the richest of fare." (Isaiah 55:1-3) Our God desires that we have the thirst to articulate the message of salvation to everyone he directs to our path.

LOST, BUT FOUND

Arleatha, age 9, had wandered off when her family was camping. The family looked everywhere for her, but to no avail. Arleatha was lost. Uppermost on the minds of her parents was whether she would ever be found. A search party was established with the sheriff and a group of 100 volunteers who combed the woods for the little girl. They shouted "Arleatha!, Where are you?" No Arleatha. It was dark, cold, and it started to rain. The search was temporarily called off. On the next day the search party heard a rustle in the woods. It was Arleatha under a tree. Safe, but cold and hungry. She had been found.

As the church-at-large we have to plan a search party to seek out the lost. We must hold hands together in unity and search until we find the lost souls. In our natural state we are lost spiritually. We were enemies of God and far from Christ. God didn't leave us in our lost condition. He sent Christ as our Savior, as the Good Shepherd, to seek and to save those who were lost. Where are our search teams? Are they active in the church?

IS WATSON BEATABLE?

In the medical field a doctor is trained to formulate a diagnosis from the symptoms that a patient exhibits. Overall, well-trained medical doctors usually do find the proper diagnosis. But there are times when they are virtually stumped because many diseases have similar symptoms. A wise doctor therefore may consult with a specialist in order to arrive at the correct diagnosis. The computer WATSON, the invention of a genius, has been employed on the quiz program Jeopardy to beat the contestants. WATSON always wins. WATSON has a storehouse of infinite information. Medical science is planning to use WATSON to make diagnoses on patients. Will medical doctors become obsolete in our technological society or will technology enhance scientific inquiry? For sure, the diagnosis will be arrived at more quickly. WATSON'S capabilities will also be humbling to the medical field.

A SPIRITUAL DIAGNOSIS

The church does not use a computer to see the depravity of man and the need for Christ as Savior. Using medical categories to arrive at a proper diagnosis of the spiritual patient we find. *SYMPTOMS*. Apathy, indifference, want to be entertained, non-committal, lack of interest.

What caused these symptoms? They include: 1) No spiritual foundation in youth. 2) Drifting away from the established church. 3) Falling away from church emotionally. 4) The lack of concern by the church-at-large. *DIAGNOSIS*. Spiritually bereft, bankrupt, sinful, enemy of God. *TREATMENT* Just as a medical diagnosis may not be well-received by a patient, so mankind doesn't like the diagnosis of their lives of sin and rebellion against God. But it is necessary for the church to point out a weak spiritual condition and that a person is eternally lost without Christ.

The Israelites in the Old Testament forgot God by substituting JAHWEH for the surrounding foreign gods. Today, a large percentage of people have forgotten God and in its place have substituted humanism (man is the measure of all things) in their lives. They suffer from a spiritual amnesia. *DIAGNOSIS*. Amnesia, the partial or total loss of memory caused by brain injury or by shock repression. Sometimes medical amnesia is permanent while sometimes it is temporary. People forget who they are, their loved ones, occupation, and friends. *TREATMENT*. Mayo Clinic utilizes the following medical modalities to treat amnesia: 1) Patient works with a therapist to learn new information that will replace the old. 2) Memory training. 3) Use smart technology to assist patients with their daily tasks. 4) No medications are used.

What is the treatment for spiritual amnesia?

REMIND THEM
1) Who they are by the grace and mercy of God.
2) That the Lord no longer recalls their sins, but washes away all past, present, and future sins through the blood of Christ.
3) The Holy Spirit, through the Word, produces a change in their hearts.
4) To RETURN BACK to God.
5) God calls forth all to repent. "I have declared to both Jews and Greeks that they must turn to God in repentance and have faith in our Lord Jesus." (Acts 20:21) "And the blood of Jesus, his Son, purifies us from all sin." (1John 1:7b)

PUTTING OUT THE FLEECE

Every pastor must equip his people to be effective in evangelism. He takes the lead to organize, mobilize, and strategize the congregation in evangelism. Gideon, one of the judges of Israel, who fought against the Midianites, put out the fleece in order to determine God's will and direction in his life. (Judges 6: 36-40) We, too, have to put out the fleece in our lives to see the direction God wishes to guide us. We search for a confirmation of our ventures, the fruition of our goal-setting and the accomplishment of our task. Gideon's name, from the Hebrew, means "tree-feller." It was Jahweh's divine plan that Gideon, a great judge of Israel, would fell the mighty armies of the Midianites. On a tour in Israel in 2011, I visited the exact site where God tested Gideon and his select band. They were chosen by the manner in which they drank the water from a pond. Gideon conquered the Midianites with just 300 men. Just think what thousands of Christians could do to spread the gospel!

OPPORTUNE TIME TO WITNESS

During my 5 years at Concordia Seminary, St. Louis, Mo. (1953-1958), I chose a different job each summer in order to meet a cross-section of humanity. One summer, I worked at a company that manufactured frozen food freezers for grocery stores. On one occasion, I was given the opportunity to witness to an ex-Lutheran, who was very confused religiously. "I don't believe in the devil" he said. I showed him from the Scriptures that the devil is a fallen angel who tries to alienate us from God. I also spoke to a janitor who said "I believe what the church believes and the church believes what I believe." With his double-talk, I again pointed him to Christ as his Savior. Be on the alert for opportunities to witness.

A BARRIER TO REMOVE

All of us on many occasions have seen how people are unrepentant. Sometimes, when they wrong a person they may say "I am sorry." But seldom, it reaches that point. To be complete, there have to be several elements of contrition. They are: I am sorry. I won't do it again. I will change my behavior. The beautiful Greek word, METANOIA, means a change of heart, repentance. Repentance takes a complete 180-degree turn. It goes further in dealing with our sin. Sin separates us from God. That barrier of sin had to be removed for reconciliation with God. This was done by the barrier-remover, Jesus Christ, who took on our sins, died, and rose from the dead, and is our personal Savior through faith. Through Christ we live changed lives. We are people with changed hearts, changed minds and changed goals in life. John the Baptist, preaching in the wilderness, said to the people of his day "Produce fruit in keeping with repentance." (Matthew 3:8) The same is true today. Repentance and the forgiveness of sins must be preached in this era. The Scriptures state "Righteousness exalts a nation, but sin is a disgrace to any people." (Proverbs 14:34)

BE YOUR OWN PERSON

Be your own person in witnessing! There is no perfect witnessing style. You must develop your own style that you feel comfortable with and practice it. It is as breathing and eating.

Many manuals have been written by all denominations to train people in evangelism. Training is vital. Memorizing Scripture is important. So many people lament and say: "I am just too old to memorize any new Scriptures. Really? No.

Col. Sanders developed his multi-million dollar KFC as a senior citizen; and a 91-year old (in great shape) completed a triathlon. It can be done. A 64-year-old woman swam from Cuba to Florida. Be comfortable in your own style of witnessing!

A DYSFUNCTIONAL CHURCH	A HEALTHY CHURCH
1. Ineffective evangelism outreach	1. Effective evangelism
2. Lip service to The Great Commission	2. Implements The Great Commission
3. No clear vision	3. Has a clear vision
4. Only supper orientation	4. A 12-week course
5. Pastor ram-rods his program	5. Vox populi
6. Lies, deception, cover ups	6. Truthful in all things
7. Alienates core members	7. Involves all members
8. Poor assimilation of the new	8. Excellent assimilation
9. Pastor's agenda is not the congregation's agenda	9. Pastor & members on same page
10. Resistant to criticism	10. Open to criticism
11. No visits by the Pastor	11. Great visitation
12. Dwindling volunteers	12. Abundant volunteers
13. Lacks flexibility	13. Open to change
14. No communication	14. Excellent communication
15. Distrustful and disunity	15. Trusting & unified
16. Talks about people	16. Discusses vital issues

17. Unstable membership
18. Closed system
19. Poorly organized
20. Digs in their heels
21. Not focused on Christ
22. No Mission statement

23. Lack basic leadership
24. Inter-generational church
25. Atmosphere of conflict
26. No follow through on plans
27. Lacks community emphasis
28. Few in Bible classes
29. Loveless
30. Ruled by a few
31. Turned inward
32. Lack of finances
33. Marginal existence
34. Hyper-critical
35. Poorly trained officers
36. Verbal fighting
37. Gossip & slander

17. Steady growth pattern
18. Open system
19. Highly organized
20. Willing to compromise
21. Focused on Christ
22. Implements mission statement

23. Broad base of leadership
24. Non-related
25. Manages conflict
26. Good follow through
27. Community involved
28. Numerous Bible classes
29. Loving & caring
30. Priesthood of believers
31. Turned outward
32. Good stewardship
33. Thriving congregation
34. Positive emphasis
35. Well-trained officers
36. Peace & harmony
37. Truthful

A CONGREGATIONAL CHECK LIST

Congregations are encouraged to check the chart entitled The Dysfunctional Church and Healthy Church and rate their individual congregation according to the following rating:

DYSFUNCTIONAL CHURCH

  1-4   Send up a S.O.S.
  5-8   Seek outside consultant
  9-11   Need help

HEALTHY CHURCH

CHAPTER TEN

BRANDED FOR CHRIST

GROWTH IN THE KINGDOM

BASILEIA TOU THEOU (Greek for "the kingdom of God") is utilized extensively in the New Testament. Jesus used this term when he introduced this parable to his disciples and the people of his day. (Luke 13: 18-21) Is the church-at-large stagnant? Is it status quo? Yes, in many ways. One of ways is in the area of evangelism. God expects growth in his kingdom. This expectation of growth is exemplified in the Parable of the Mustard Seed in Matthew 13. The mustard seed, the leaven, and the fishing net depict the expectation of kingdom growth. The mustard seed is smallest of all seeds, but when planted and nourished, grows to be a huge mustard tree with many branches.

Leaven or yeast is also utilized to denote growth. When yeast is placed in dough, the dough rises. God wants us to be mustard seeds and yeast in this world. Strategically-placed growth is inevitable in God's kingdom.

A BUMPY RIDE

There are times in church work, especially in evangelism, when the marching order always comes from Jesus our Commander-in-Chief. "Saddle up! Let's ride!" But before we can ride a horse, we have to have the saddle on properly, making sure the cinctures are firm and the bridle is ready. At times, the ride may be a bumpy ride. We encounter barriers and obstacles we never thought we would experience. There must be preparedness in evangelism. "Giddy up" to our horse to move ahead. There are times when we must say "WHOA" to rethink and recalculate our evangelism plan in the congregation. When there is a Spanish horse, we would give the command, "Vamanos! or "Alto!"

CHRIST'S ATONING LOVE

As Christians in our witnessing, we must have the clear facts to deliver and present the message of salvation, in a loving and effective manner. We are so undeserving of God's love. Yet, in love, God sent his only-begotten Son to die for us. "We love him because he first loved us." (1 John 4:19) "He is the atoning[1] sacrifice for our sins, and not only for ours but also for the sins of the whole world." (1 John 2:2)

THE MAGNETISM OF THE CROSS

We speak of Types and Anti-Types in Biblical exegesis. In Numbers 21:4-9, Moses placed a bronze serpent upon a pole and all of the Israelites, who looked in faith, were healed. This is an Old Testament type of Christ. In the New Testament Anti-Type in John 3:14,15, Jesus says "Just as Moses lifted up the snake in the desert, so the Son of Man must be lifted up, that everyone who believes in him may have eternal life." The cross of Christ is a magnet that draws people to the death and crucifixion of our Lord. Christ has that power to pull people toward him in love and forgiveness. May we radiate the love of Christ and point people to the death and resurrection of Jesus Christ, who gave his life that we may have eternal life!

A NEW WARDROBE

Style means everything to many people. People will go to great lengths to wear the most fashionable clothing. The New York City Garment

District is a busy place where the latest fashions are transported to the airport for distribution to all parts of the world. Fashion designers always want to present their latest fall and spring lines of clothing by engaging the best models to model their clothing. Living in Chicago, our oldest son, Todd, had a great talent for tennis and practiced a lot. Clothed in his tattered outfit, he won his matches. Steve, our other son, told him "Todd, you have to be fashionable and get a different outfit!" When he did, he lost all of his games. Todd, not concerned with fashion, would go to a clothing store and say to the clerk" I'll buy the style on the mannequin." The adage "clothes make the man" doesn't apply in reference to our spiritual state. Paul relates what our former life was when we followed the dictates of the Old Man. They include deceitful lusts, lying stealing, anger and evil communications. Although we still are tempted and still commit these sins, Paul clinches it, "And to put on the new self, created to be like God in true righteousness and holiness." (Ephesians 4:22-32) Sin is the shroud of corruption, and not fashionable. Spiritual togs in our life of sanctification are always in style.

THE MARK OF OUR BAPTISM

"You are all sons of God through faith in Christ Jesus, for all of you who were baptized into Christ have clothed yourselves with Christ." (Galatians 3:26-27) By the holy sacrament of Baptism, the Holy Spirit, in the water and Word, made us God's own by faith. Faith was created in the hearts of infants at infant baptism. Christian sponsors spoke on behalf of the infant. On the day of their confirmation, teenagers renew their baptismal promise that was made at their baptism. "Fear not, for I have redeemed you, I have called by your name. You are Mine." (Isaiah 43:1) We belong to our Lord, not only by Christ's redemption, but by a divine mark placed upon us. He has called us by name, guaranteeing that we belong to him as a choice possession. Our Lutheran Agenda's baptismal service states "Receive the sign of the holy cross both upon your forehead and upon your heart to mark you as one redeemed by Christ the crucified." Our baptism reminds us of being "branded" by Christ in several ways: 1) A daily reminder that we have been regenerated by the Holy Spirit and made a child of God. 2) A daily incentive to drown the Old Man in our lives that the New Man in Christ will be evident. Sad to say that the adage of the world is: HATCHED! MATCHED! DISPATCHED!

OPEN DOORS FOR WITNESSING

John, the apostle, writes to the church at Philadelphia "I know your deeds. See, I have placed before you an open door that no one can shut." (Revelation 3:8) These are words of encouragement from God who is Alpha and Omega. Philadelphia was the only church of the seven churches of Asia Minor, where Christ commended them for their performance of spreading the Word. Today, God opens doors in all of our churches and in the myriad of lives. When God opens a door--don't close it because of stubbornness or neglect. Walk through that door, and in faith see where the Lord desires to take you. We are by nature controlling people. We want to be in control of everything. Allow God the Holy Spirit to guide you and be controlled by his direction. By our sins, we close the doors to witnessing and missions. When God closes doors he also opens other doors of opportunity.

In 2012, I toured Greece, Turkey, and Rome. We visited the island of Patmos where St. John the Divine was banished; and where, under verbal inspiration, he penned the book of Revelation. His domicile was a cave grotto reachable via winding stairs. We also toured the museum at the top of the monastery on the island. Think of the open doors God gives each of us daily! There are millions of people hurting due to their sins. They do not know where to turn for direction. Too often, they turn to the cults and other groups, instead of churches preaching Christ and him crucified. Possibly you have been through such a tragic situation, a loss of a loved one, or a child who committed suicide. God will use you to relate in a one-to-one way to that person who is suffering from that loss. Christianity is faith-in-action. Too often, people are wobbly recruits with no direction. Pastors, as the head of evangelism, must train the troops for action.

NO RETREAT

When Cortez dispatched his last command to his men "Burn the boats!" there was no chance for retreat. They couldn't return home in their own boats, but only in the boats of the conquered. In July 1863, Colonel Joshua Chamberlain, of the Union Army, led his troops at the Battle of Gettysburg at Little Round Top. His army had exhausted all of their ammunition. He realized the success of the war hinged on holding the left flank at all costs. He commanded his men "Load your bayonets—charge!" They won the battle. He became a general after the Civil War. For him there was no retreat. So it should be for Christians in witnessing. The devil wants us to give up and retreat from battle. But we must press on-- charge!

ENLARGE AND STRENGTHEN

A renowned artist mentored many painters. One artist, with great potential, brought his painting to his master. Without saying a word, the master artist wrote on the painting "amplius" meaning amplify, enlarge. Isaiah the prophet says: "Enlarge the place of your tent, stretch out your tent curtains wide, do not hold back; lengthen your cords, strengthen your stakes." (Isaiah 54:2) As Isaiah gave the mandate to his people, he directs us to do so in our congregations today. The Israelites could identify with the metaphor of a tent, for they were a nomadic people for many years. Even the tabernacle, when they encamped, was a huge tent. We are directed not only to move out in faith to strengthen the gospel message, but at the same time, to strengthen our present structure. Most of the time, church work does not hum on all 8 cylinders at the same time. Other programs have their down time.

DISCIPLESHIP

There was a woman who complained about the cross she had to bear. One night, she dreamed that she threw her cross onto a pile of other crosses and picked out a different cross. She said, "This cross is too light." She picked another and said, "This one is too heavy." She picked up a third cross and said "This one is just right." Here she picked up the original one she had discarded. Our heavenly Father knows what he is doing when he assigns a cross for us to bear. We may moan and complain, but it is God's gracious dealing with us in our lives. Sometimes, only in eternity, will we know the real purpose of the cross that we have to bear. Will you accept this gracious branding by your Lord and be a cross-bearer for Jesus?

Joni Tade is a marvelous example of a Christian with a cross to bear, due to a swimming accident paralyzing her from the waist down. Yet, she has written books and appeared on religious programs attesting to the greatness of her God. What a witness for Jesus Christ! Jesus never promised that life would be easy when you become a Christian and remain faithful to Him. There are trials, sicknesses, disappointments, vicissitudes, sorrows, hospitalization, and tribulation. "See, I have refined you, though not as silver; I have tested you in the furnace of all affliction." (Isaiah 48:10) Metallurgists refine gold and silver, exposing the metal to more intense heat, which separates the precious metal from the dross. Maybe, there is just too much dross in our lives, that has to be purified. Will you accept this branding or will you rebel against the Divine Metallurgist, as he touches you with his love?

CROSS-BEARING FOR CHRIST

Branding may lead to cross-bearing for Christ. What is a cross? What does it mean to be a cross-bearer, as we follow Christ? Too often, we regard everything that happens in our lives as a cross to bear. Due to sin in general, there are discouragements and failures along the road of life. But these items do not constitute a cross. A cross, clearly defined, is anything a Christian suffers, because they profess Christ as their Savior. The cross may take the forms of persecution and death in other parts of the world; while in the United States, it could be scorn and ridicule. The events that happen to unbelievers are direct punishment for their sins. For Christians, it is a loving chastisement from our God. (Hebrews 12: 7-10; 1 Corinthians 11:32)

What are some reasons for loving reprimands from our God?

+ HUMBLE US. (James 4:10)
+ TEST OUR FAITH. (I Peter 1:6-7)
+ DEVELOP PATIENCE UNDER DURESS. (Romans 12:2)
+ HELP US TO DENY WORLDLY LUSTS. (I Peter 4:1,2)
+ ENCOURAGE US TO SEEK OUR LORD IN PRAYER. (Isaiah 26:16)
+ KEEP OUR EYES ON SPIRITUAL, NOT EARTHLY ITEMS. (2 Corinthians 4:16-18)
+ REVEAL A TOKEN OF GOD'S LOVE FOR CHRISTIANS. (Hebrews 12:6)
+ EQUIP US TO SERVE OTHERS. (2 Timothy 3:17)
+ DRAW US CLOSER TO GOD. (Psalm 16:11)
+ DIRECTS US TO ASK "WHAT IS THE LORD TRYING TO TELL ME THROUGH THIS EXPERIENCE?" (Proverbs 3:11)
+ REMIND US THAT WE HAVE BEEN BRANDED BY CHRIST. (Matthew 16:24)
+ PROMPT US THAT ONLY HEAVEN WILL REVEAL THE REAL REASON FOR THIS CROSS (Jude: 24)

DO YOU HAVE THE RIGHT MARK?

Tattoos are the rage among 18- 34 year olds. People display them on all parts of their anatomy. Many pride themselves that their tattoo is very unique and never will be replicated. Tattoos are quite evident on almost all of the professional basketball players. It seems to be a mark of importance or a cry for attention. Tattoo parlors have sprung up all over America; and tattoos are expensive, painful when applied, and expensive to remove them. Tattoos do make a statement; and you wonder what is that statement? If a tattoo (consisting of a symbol of various colored dyes) means so much to people, how much more should the spiritual mark Christ places upon the Christian mean? The Christian has the mark of love, concern, empathy, and zeal to tell others of salvation through the merits of Jesus Christ.

CRUCIFIED WITH CHRIST

Paul, the veteran of the cross, states "I have been crucified with Christ and I no longer live, but Christ lives in me. The life I live in the body, I live by faith in the Son of God, who loved me and gave himself for me." (Galatians 2:20) What a test of faith by the Apostle Paul! Can we make such a bold confession of faith? I hope so. Crucifixion means death and agony. Are we willing to suffer all for the sake of the gospel, in order to tell someone about Christ?

RELATIONSHIP WITH JESUS CHRIST

We have to ask ourselves the heart-searching question "What is my relationship to Jesus Christ?" Rescuer? Friend? Lord? Savior? Redeemer? Shepherd? Yes, and more in the everyday life of a Christian. Christ must be not only Christo-centric in our own lives, but is necessary for us to pass it on to the unchurched. Who does the world see through you? If it is only YOU, then our evangelism efforts have failed. But if the love of Christ is radiated, people will see Christ. Paul, reminds us "So then, just as you received Christ Jesus as Lord, continue to live in him, rooted and built up in him, strengthened in the faith, as you were taught, and overflowing with thankfulness." (Colossians 2: 6, 7)

FISHERS OF MEN

Another Scriptural appellation for Christians is "fishers of men." When Jesus called Peter and Andrew as His disciples he said, "Come, follow me, and I will make you fishers of men." (Matthew 4:9)

Jesus also called James and John as his disciples. Notice in the Bible that immediately they followed him. What about the Christian world today? Is their reaction like the Expedia's TV commercial, offering a free trip NOW with immediate travel? Most had excuses. "I can't today" "I have too many things scheduled." One person accepted and traveled to his land of dreams in China. Are you a follower of Jesus Christ? Will you go at a moment's notice to serve your God?

Decades ago, Christians wore fishhooks on their lapels, denoting and reminding themselves that they were fishers of men. It was also a conversational piece to talk to a person about Christ.

John 21:1-6 records the biblical account of the huge draught of fish caught by the disciples following Jesus's command. They hauled in 153 fish. What a haul! Let's go fishing and catch men!

On a 2011 Holy Land tour, our group visited the Sea of Galilee[2] and boarded a ship similar to what Jesus and his disciples sailed in biblical days. The captain demonstrated how the early disciples would cast their nets. What do you expect when you cast your spiritual nets in your everyday conversations with individuals? Do you expect minnows or big catfish? What are your expectations when you cast out your net? The devil attempts to dissuade us by whispering in our ears "Your effort is useless-- you won't catch anyone." Too often we succumb and fail to cast out our nets. We must cast our nets with great boldness, trusting that the Lord will bless our endeavors. Are you willing to take the risk? We, as human beings, take risks everyday of our lives. Every time we drive our car, there is a risk we could be in a fender-bender or worse.

THE BEACON OF THE CROSS STILL SHINES

September 11, 2001 was horrific in the history books of the United States, when the Twin Towers of the World Trade Center, New York City were hit by two planes of terrorists taking the innocent lives of thousands. But America came back stronger than ever by building a more functional and beautiful World Trade Center during these past years. Over 1,200 workers have been employed to build this new structure that towers high amid the skyline of New York City.

After the recovery period, the clean up of the debris from the old towers began. Then new towers were built with a retaining wall surrounding them like a bathtub to block the water of the Hudson River. Debris and water was filling up this containment. It had to be rectified. As debris was cleared and reinforcing concrete was poured, the workers found something very interesting in the wreckage. When the smoke and dust cleared, there was two pieces of steel fashioned as a cross. Some say it was an accident. For Christians, the cross is a symbol of redemption and a reminder that Christ died for the sins of the world, and rose victorious on Easter morn. The hymn writer pens the familiar words:

> In the cross of Christ I glory,
> Tow'ring o'er the wrecks of time.
> All the light of sacred story
> Gathers round its head sublime.

The cross arose as a phoenix out of the ashes of the destroyed World Trade Center. In 2011, the museum was opened to the public. The outer courtyard was surrounded by a waterfall and trees, and displayed plaques with names of all the deceased. The deceased not only include the thousands who perished at the Twin Towers, but also those who died at Shanks, Pennsylvania. On September 11, 2013, a beacon consisting of patriotic red, white, and blue colors was lit, sending beams of freedom, liberty, encouragement, and remembrance throughout New York City. As this light serves as a beacon, so does the beacon of God's love envelope the world with his arms of grace, calling the world to repentance and faith. But is the Christian church the beacon light as God intended it to be? The devil and the world try to snuff out this gospel light. As Christians we can't allow this to happen. Let us be beacons that shine in darkness pointing people to Christ. This is accomplished by a relational-type of evangelism on a one-on-one basis.

ANDREW THE APOSTLE

Andrew[3] the apostle is recognized as an evangelist who brought his brother Peter to Jesus. The apostle put personal evangelism into action. (John 1:41, 42) John the Baptist, harbinger of Christ, prepared John, Andrew, Peter, Philip, and Nathaniel for the ministry of Jesus. The disciples of our Lord took The Great Commission very seriously when they preached the pure gospel making disciples of all nations. Where did Andrew concentrate his ministry? He preached along the Black Sea and the Dnieper River as far as Kiev and then to Novgorod[4]. How did Andrew meet his demise? He was crucified in Pat as in Achaea on a X-shaped cross (crux decussata or saltire)[5] which is called the Saint Andrews Cross. The liturgical churches, namely Lutheran, Roman Catholic, Episcopal, and Presbyterian observe St. Andrew the Apostle Day on November 30. Let us emulate Andrew who demonstrates the personal zeal of witnessing and winsome style of evangelism! We must utilize that personal technique of reaching out to others on a one-to-one basis.

NOTES

[1] The Greek word is HILASMOS, denoting propitiation. God gives mercy to sinners who believe in the expiatory sacrifice of Christ.

[2] The Sea of Galilee is often referred to in the Bible as the Lake of Gennesaret (Luke 5:1) and as the Sea of Tiberias. (John 21:1)

[3] His name is from the Greek ANDREIA, meaning manhood, valor. Andrew appears to be a common name in biblical times.

[4] He became a patron saint of Scotland, Romania, and Russia. Some scholars state that Andrew established the See of Byzantium (Constantinople) in 38 A.D. Basil of Seleucia knew Andrew's mission in Thrace along with Scythia and Achaia. *Encyclopedia of Early Christianity*, Ferguson, Everett, p. 51.

[5] According to legend, Oengus II in 832 A. D. led his army of Scots and Picts into a battle against Angles. Through outnumbered, he vowed that if God would deliver him the victory, he would make Saint Andrew the Patron Saint of Scotland. Oengus was victorious and he kept his vow. Today, a background of blue with an X cross is the national flag of Scotland. *History of the Abbey and Palace of Holyroodhouse* Parker Larson, John (1848), p. 169.

CHAPTER ELEVEN

CHANGING SCENES ON THE PRAIRIE: A NATIONAL SURVEY

The cowboy certainly is amazed at the changing scenes along the trail that he may encounter. One time the wind can rattle your bones with cold, while a dust storm could cloud the way of the trail. On some trails there will be tumbleweeds, while on others cacti. The trail is always changing. Sometimes, the vegetation may change on the trail. In the Southwest portion of our United States and parts of Mexico, the Saguaro cactus is indigenous. A spring rain changes the desert. The cacti blossoms forth in its splendor and glory with the spring rains.

Isaiah the prophet declares: "The desert and the parched land will be glad; the wilderness will rejoice and blossom. Like the crocus, it will burst into bloom; it will rejoice greatly and shout for joy. The glory of Lebanon will be given to it, the splendor of Carmel and Sharon; they will see the glory of the Lord, the splendor of our God." (Isaiah 35:1-2) As human beings, we are subject to changes all around us. But it is most comforting to know that we have one who is changeless—Christ. "I, the Lord do not change" (Malachi 3:6a) "I am Alpha and the Omega." (Revelation 1: 8a)

The world is changing so rapidly that the church should be one step ahead of the world. I can certainly attest to this. In one of my ministries, I served Christ Lutheran of Logan Square, Chicago,

Illinois. This was an inner-city congregation with a target outreach to the Hispanic population. The church had 650 communicants with a day school of 150 students. Our goals to reach the Hispanics included: 1) The school nurtured their faith and involved households. 2) English as a second language classes were offered. 3) Spanish was learned by the gringos. 4) Parent Teacher League met monthly. 5) A Spanish Pastor was called to conduct Sunday worship services and minister to the pastoral needs of the Hispanic community. I spent a month at Escuela de Lingua, Cuernavaca, Mexico to study Spanish. The area pastors met weekly to learn Spanish taught by a Spanish-speaking teacher.

During this time, class consciousness and its effects were observed among Mexicans, Puerto Ricans, and Cubans, and Hispanics from South America. The mission theme was A CHANGELESS CHRIST FOR A CHANGING COMMUNITY. "Jesus Christ is the same yesterday and today and forever." (Hebrews 13:8)

A national survey was sent out to Pastors of Lutheran, Methodist, Baptist, Presbyterian, and Episcopal churches to gleam and record how these churches (as a sampling) deal with and implement evangelism in their respective churches.

The following is the recorded data.

THE NATIONAL SURVEY OF EVANGELISM

Pastor, when you complete this survey, please fill in the blanks:
Denomination _____ Size of congregation _____
East _____ West _____ North _____ South _____ Mid-West _____

1) How does your congregation implement The Great Commission?

2) My congregation is: Interested ____ Disinterested _____ or Ignores _____ the topic of evangelism.

3) Evangelism is an integral part of our annual budget. We allocate $ _____ per year for evangelism.

4) As Pastor, I train my people for outreach into the community.
YES ____ NO ____.

5) I feel the following are obstacles for an effective evangelism program:
1.
2.
3.

6) The following programs have been successful for an outreach into our community:
1.
2.
3.

7) Due to the large size of my congregation, I have delegated the role of evangelism to: Associate Pastor _____Teacher _____Director of Evangelism _____ Lay person ____

8) It has been difficult to enroll lay people on my Outreach Board due to _____.

9) I have found the following effective avenues to enlist board members for evangelism:
1.
2.
3.

10) My congregation has been effective in outreach to the following groups in a specific way:
1. Boomers

2. Busters

3. Millennials

4. Mosaics

Here are the salient data of Lutheran, Presbyterian, Baptist, Methodist, and Episcopal congregations, who responded.

LUTHERAN
SIZE: 70-3,000 members.

LOCATION: Mid-West predominantly, where Lutheranism is strong. Some from North, East, and West.

PRESBYTERIAN
SIZE: 75-1,000 members.

LOCATION: Mid-West, South, East. Predominantly East

BAPTIST
SIZE: 75 to 24,000 members.

LOCATION: North, South, West

METHODIST
SIZE: 50 to 1,300 members.

LOCATION: Mid-West; West. South

EPISCOPAL
SIZE: 75 to 600 members.

LOCATION: South, East, West

The following are the responses from the different denominations to the national survey questions.

1) HOW DOES YOUR CONGREGATION IMPLEMENT THE GREAT COMMISSION?

LUTHERAN
In our mission statement; to make and grow disciples; equipping people to articulate the truth in vibrant ways; individual sharing; relationship building; small group outreach; outreach from our school; Garden Ministry; Food Bank; service; Live and share the gospel; inviting the community; missions and missionaries.

PRESBYTERIAN
Website, ROKU; local TV broadcast; door-to-door canvassing; community events; missions; Vacation Bible School; proclamation of the gospel; fellowship, worship, witness Alpha Course.

BAPTIST
Co-operative program; global outreach and missions; we train our people to use the faith program in sharing the gospel; make disciples; service projects; relational evangelism training; prayer; youth groups; church programs; pulpit messages.

METHODIST
Personal testimonies; outreach; preschool.
The Great Commission is our #1 priority to the unchurched in the community; connecting with community members; and the sharing of the Good News of the gospel.

EPISCOPAL
Personal invitation; fellowship; outreach to the community; neighborhood outreach to homeless, food bank; and new members welcome plan.

My CONGREGATION IS: INTERESTED _____
DISINTERESTED _____ OR IGNORES _____ THE TOPIC OF EVANGELISM.

LUTHERAN
The consensus of the reporting congregations is that they are interested.

PRESBYTERIAN
They are interested in evangelism.

BAPTIST
They are interested in evangelism.

METHODIST
They are interested in evangelism.

EPISCOPAL
They are interested in evangelism.

3) EVANGELISM IS AN INTEGRAL PART OF OUR BUDGE WE $ _____ PER YEAR FOR EVANGELISM.

LUTHERAN
Ranges from $1,000.00 to $10,000.00.

PRESBYTERIAN
Range from $1,000.00 to $15,000.00.

BAPTIST
Ranges from $5,000 to $54,000.00

METHODIST
Ranges from 0 to 10% of annual budget.

EPISCOPAL
$500.00 to 10% of budget.

4) AS PASTOR, I TRAIN MY PEOPLE FOR OUTREACH INTO THE COMMUNITY.

LUTHERAN
In the congregations reporting, the Pastor trains his people. There was 1 "no" answer.

PRESBYTERIAN
All yes, except 1 "no" from an Interim Pastor.

BAPTIST
All trained by the Pastor.

METHODIST
All reporting said "yes."

EPISCOPAL
Yes, except for 1 "no" from Interim Pastor.

5) I FEEL THE FOLLOWING ARE OBSTACLES FOR AN EFFECTIVE EVANGELISM PROGRAM

LUTHERAN
Apathy of Pastors and people; too many other concerns; church stigma; people see it as a program, not as a lifestyle; too busy; lack of friends in non-Christian community; feeling it is the Pastor's job; lack of community involvement; changing culture; lack of clarity of what it means to be a Jesus-follower; church's failure to train people to a total responsibility for reaching the lost; lack of practice at talking about their everyday faith in Christ; Pastors unwilling to invest energy in outreach; Christians being afraid; lack of receptive listeners; not having one set time for calls; inexperience in telling own gospel story; fear of anti-Christian culture & multi-cultural community; large church-going community; no good programs to model; our community is in a rapid ethnic change.

PRESBYTERIAN
Fear of rejection; disinterest; small numbers; congregation members over 90 and some under 50); ignorance; past situations that had bad results; feelings of inadequacies; lack of spirit; timidity.

BAPTIST

Anti-Christian culture; religious environment dominated by Catholicism; fear of sharing the gospel; wrong concept of "the world doesn't want to know"; laity not trained to witness; do not have the confidence to share; gated communities; people scared to open their doors to strangers; people are distant in church; not understanding local needs; seeing evangelism as a program rather than a lifestyle.

METHODIST

Old images of evangelism outreach methods; embarrassment; fear of engaging strangers and even neighbors; the idea that in the West, we don't do that; uniformed; some pastors do not personally witness and practice evangelism; it seems to be a low priority with church members; many members have not been trained in evangelism; fear of offending another person; lack of theological understanding; lack of effective training; lack of member's ability to tell their story.

EPISCOPAL

Uncertainty; fear; lack of leadership; lack of demographic info; money; time; lack of cultural acceptance; anti-Christian mind-set; competition for time; busy families.

6) THE FOLLOWING PROGRAMS HAVE BEEN SUCCESSFUL FOR AN OUTREACH INTO OUR COMMUNITY

LUTHERAN

Meeting felt needs; personal invitation; warm and welcoming environment; day school; followup calls, cards and visits to visitors; radio, TV and postcards for public relations; community service projects; ministry to street people; Bible groups; prayer walks; community involvement both on and off campus; Child Development Center; members stepping into their neighbors lives; Alternative Life Groups; computerized lighted road signs; newspaper, postcard mailings and personal invitation cards for members to hand out;

reaching out to the apartment managers, using Mover mailings; food pantry; recovery ministry; preschool; school; official Pastoral acts to non-members; large school draws members, preschool is a feeder; social ministry projects; Big Days of Service (twice a year emphasis on serving the unchurched); Jesus Hands; Open Arms Child Care Center; building long-term friendships; welcome kits; free coffee in front of our building; bridging Hispanic mission outreach; backpack ministry; television ministry; praise band.

PRESBYTERIAN

Community events, door-to-door canvasses; Alpha, Explore Go; community garden (400 pounds of vegetables;) shelters; Hunger Action; Elderly Ministry; mid-week fellowship with a meal; monthly picnic, ice cream socials; mission projects; media; personal invitation.

BAPTIST

Alta programs; Strategic Partners based on Acts 1:8; serving our community; energetic worship services; casual atmosphere; community carnival for children in our community; mail, e-mail, informational neighborhood invitation for special events; evangelistic emphasis on Sundays; special events; one-on-one evangelism to family; dramas.

METHODIST

Part-time classes; Ecumenical worship services; Bring-A-Friend-Sunday; musical concerts; community service days; evangelism by evening sermons; jazz concerts; Alpha Class; confrontational evangelism; every event includes evangelism; Kids Hope USA; food banks; garden; prayer books to the community; uniform closet.

EPISCOPAL

Praise services; food; working with inter-faith project for the homeless; Habitat for Humanity; Lenten Fish Fry; presence in the community; Episcopal School.

7) DUE TO THE LARGE SIZE OF MY CONGREGATION, I HAVE DELEGATED THE ROLE OF EVANGELISM TO: ASSOCIATE PASTOR _____TEACHER _____ DIRECTOR OF EVANGELISM _____LAY PERSON _____

LUTHERAN

Pastor, Associate Pastor, layperson, all of the staff; teacher; Outreach Coordinator. However, Senior Pastor has the primary responsibility for the whole ministry with a team priority; every member is a witness; as the Pastor, I take the lead, but I share it with every leader and member. In the large congregations, the Associate Pastor has the leading role in evangelism.

PRESBYTERIAN

As Pastor, I am in charge. I do not delegate. All staff persons participate; Lay persons.

BAPTIST

A team effort; tried to delegate, but delegation failed. Outreach Pastor for evangelism; Pastor is is responsible.

METHODIST

Assisted by the laity; all are responsible; Associate Pastor; teacher; lay person.

EPISCOPAL

Lay Person who functions as Newcomer Minister and director of communications; Outreach Committee; clergy and laity.

8) IT IS DIFFICULT TO ENROLL LAY PEOPLE ON MY OUTREACH BOARD DUE TO _____.

LUTHERAN
Members feel it is staff's role; disconnect of age, ethnicity, social/ economic position between the congregation members and the surrounding community; we do not have board. No board, but a group of outreach ministries; we found that a board implies only a few people need to do evangelism; apathy; not difficult; fear; board fails to build a team effort in evangelism.

PRESBYTERIAN
Fear; indifference; we have an active board; some are uncomfortable with evangelism.

BAPTIST
Age of members; fear of not knowing what to say; not difficult when we realize the real purpose of evangelism; busy schedules; apathy.

EPISCOPAL
Members are overcommitted in church work; fear that they will be in charge and held accountable; too difficult; busy schedules.

9) I HAVE FOUND THE FOLLOWING EFFECTIVE AVENUES TO ENLIST BOARD MEMBERS FOR EVANGELISM

LUTHERAN
One-on-one invitation, person-to-person; personal modeling, training, and turning all activities into welcoming opportunities for strength; encouragement provides avenues to tell their stories; match spiritual gifts to tasks; bite-size and varied roles and tasks; short-term assignments; I don't want board members; I want us relating deeply to the members' needs and giftedness; invite members to lead something; trust the Holy Spirit to work through the Word and

assure our people of this fact; ask to serve on a person-to-person basis; make the meetings fun; not difficult; real life experiences; life-changing testimonies; sermon; and volunteers.

PRESBYTERIAN

Sharing the vision; Bible study series on evangelism; outreach programs that minister to the needs of people in the community; discussing our call to be an evangelist; select people who have the gift for evangelism; one-on-one; deacon and session leadership expectations.

BAPTIST

On-the-job training; specific people invited to pray for lost people to realize evangelism awareness and urgency in their lives; plain and simple gospel presentation; preaching about evangelism; personal request; sharing personal testimony; realize that the Holy Spirit does the work; make evangelism a part of your personal life; church-wide prayer emphasis for evangelism; training in evangelism.

METHODIST

Specific short-term assignments; mentors; Faith Friends for new members; evangelism must be a lifestyle for a Christian; classes; stewardship training and preaching; we have 25 people to be baptized; lack of evangelism small group study; ask them to be specific; we have evangelism teams.

EPISCOPAL

We need lay leaders who are really committed to enlist others; vision; telling the story of the importance of evangelism; I tell them I will pray with them; invite them to a meal; reassure them; personal contact.

10) MY CONGREGATION HAS BEEN EFFECTIVE IN THE OUTREACH TO THE FOLLOWING GROUPS IN A SPECIFIC WAY:

1. BOOMERS
2. BUSTERS
3. MILLENNIALS
4. MOSAICS

LUTHERAN

BOOMERS. For us age differences are not as significant as ethnicity and social/economic differences. Boomers are already here; invitation to worship; they love contemporary worship; mid-size communities; we welcome youth who, but we do not reach out to them; television ministry; Seniors Ministry.

BUSTERS. Ministries for their kids; through the school---they have many enrolled; family- focused programs in our bedroom community; contemporary worship; work projects.

MILLENNIALS. Specific tasks; service projects; ministries for kids; our future full-time pastors are from this generation; opportunities to reach singles; contemporary services; day school; fellowship events; our Wedding Ministry has reached many.

MOSAICS. Looking to start a new worship style; currently doing three traditional and three contemporary worship services; bringing in couples as members; clear gospel message; loving people; relational evangelism.

PRESBYTERIAN

BOOMERS. We have effective ministries to this group which include coordinated visits to nursing homes, retirement homes, and a new course we teach on growing old with dignity and grace.

BUSTERS. TV broadcasts; we have begun a new family ministry program.

MILLENNIALS. Intentional inter-generational groups.

MOSAICS. No programs.

BAPTIST

BOOMERS. Home visits; relaxed atmosphere at worship; contemporary style worship; practical Biblical preaching.

BUSTERS. Home visits; emphasis upon programs and events for children and families.

MILLENNIALS. Program and events for children and families; dramas; events.

MOSAICS. No report.

METHODIST

BOOMERS. Special worship services; Elder Ministries; Nursing home worship.

BUSTERS. Involvement in ministry.

MILLENNIALS. Mission projects.

MOSAICS. Opportunities to serve.

EPISCOPAL

BOOMERS. Lay ministry; Leadership roles due to maturity and their experiences in church work.

BUSTERS. Children and family ministry; Christian Day School.

MILLENNIALS. Children and family ministries; campus ministry.

MOSAICS. Young adult ministry; campus ministry; new youth programs.

SUMMATION

Several of the various denominations are reaching out to the Boomers, Busters, Millennials, and Mosaics. Due to the fact that the Mosaics is a fairly new category, there is and will be a great amount of experimentation and field work to be done in this group. This is the challenge now, as in all other generations, to reach the very young people who are drifting away from the established church. The congregations in the various denominations, namely Lutheran, Presbyterian, Baptist, Methodist, and Episcopal that have responded to this national survey, indicate that the church-at-large is alive and formulating new plans, events, and programs, to meet the spiritual needs of all four categories.

CHAPTER TWELVE

THE LAST ROUND-UP

ESCHATOLOGY AND THE WORLD

The doctrine of Eschatology, ESCHATOS, Greek, denoting "last things" embraces such topics as: 1) Temporal Death 2) Second Advent of Christ 3) The Resurrection of the Dead 4) The Final Judgement 5) The End of the World 6) Eternal Damnation and 7) Eternal Life.

Through Bible classes, seminars, and sermons, most Christians know the terminology and banter the nomenclature around in their conversations. Few fully realize the total import as applied to evangelism. Just pick up a copy of the The New York Times and view the theatre page; and you will be amazed at the number of plays that are playing both on Broadway and off- Broadway. Many of the plays never make the long haul. Some plays run for years on Broadway. But there is the FINAL CURTAIN for all plays.

On Judgment Day, when Jesus shall appear in His paraousia[1] there will be the absolute final curtain call. What is the Christian church-at-large doing to spread the Word and articulate the faith? Some are using all of their resources at their disposal to spread the Word, while still others are unconcerned in a malaise of lethargy. What is the cause or better yet, who is the causing agent? It is none other than the Great Saboteur known as Satan who whispers in the ear of the church, "Oh, you have plenty of time to articulate the gospel or to tell others of Christ's love." "Its not your job---let someone else do the job." "You can't afford evangelism in your church budget." These, and other lies, are perpetuated by the Father of Lies---the the devil, who is a fallen angel who seeks our eternal ruin.

As Christians, we must arm ourselves with the whole armor of God. (Ephesians 6:10-18) What happens to every human being at the point of death? At death, God judges the soul. The soul of the believer who has Christ as their Savior goes to heaven and the soul of the unbeliever to hell. Both bodies rest in the bosom of the earth to await the Day of Resurrection. The church must come to the realization of the urgency of spreading the gospel. "I tell you, now is the time of God's favor, now is the day of salvation." (2 Corinthians 6:2b)

> Hark! the voice of Jesus crying
> "Who will go and work today?
> Fields are white and harvest waiting,
> Who will bear the sheaves away?"
> Loud and long the Master calleth,
> Rich reward He offers thee;
> Who will answer, gladly saying,
> "Here am I, send me, send me"?

THE CUTTING OUT PROCESS

So often we picture the American cowboy in a cattle drive. Cattle are not driven, but trailed. There are two round-ups per year: the first round-up entails the calf round-up and branding; and the second is the "beef round-up," where the herd is prepared for shipping to market. The Judas Steer[2] was vital. This would be the time of the branding of the late calves. Cowboys were highly organized. They appointed a "round-up captain," who in turn, supervised men under him to ride the range, seeking out cattle who had strayed from the herd. They would then gather the strays to a "parade grounds" or "holding spot." Then the "cutting out" process began: the cattle were divided from the herd and driven before the "tally man." He spotted the brands and distributed them among the holding spots, according to the respective ranch.

Cowboys prized their herds, for they were their livelihood. Consequently, they had several watch periods. Cock-tail watch covered the morning hours. Killpecker watch was from sundown to 8a.m. Graveyard started at 1 a.m. Relief men who relieved the previous guard. When fences were erected, the open range and the usual round-up became history. All of these facts are important as we apply it to some salient truths of evangelism. Judgment Day is God's final Round-Up, when Christ shall appear with all his holy angels. In Matthew 25: 31-46, Jesus relates the separation of the sheep from the goats. Truly, there will be a "cutting out" process by our eternal Lord. This is faith-in-action, and has nothing to do with saved by works as some believe. It is purely by grace in Christ. Good works are the fruit of faith.

A chancel skit was presented by youth at a church. The skit depicted the beggar asking for food, the prisoner desiring visits, and naked people in need of clothing. The title of the skit was "Seeing Jesus Today." The actors claimed they didn't see Jesus in these people and missed the point of Matthew 25.

JUDGMENT DAY

No one knows the time, nor the day when Judgment Day will occur. West coast groups directed their followers to sit on the top of a hill to await Judgment Day, which never came. "Behold, I come like a thief!" (Revelation 16:15a) The Parable of Ten Virgins also illustrates this wait. (Matthew 25: 1-13) As cowboys stood guard over their herd at night, so our God sends His holy angels to guard us and encompass us with the wings of protection everyday of our lives. "For he will command his angels concerning you to guard you in all your ways. (Psalm 91:11) Time is fleeting. We do not know the hour of the final curtain call on this earth. "Be prepared" not only is a good Boy Scout motto, but necessary for vigilance, as we await the last Round-Up, when our Lord shall appear in the heavens.

FOREVER

Life is transitory. Our terra firma isn't so firm after all. It is pretty shaky with shifting sand. The Psalmist states: "Lord, teach us to number our days aright, that we may gain a heart of wisdom."

(Psalm 90:12) We are Christians today only and solely, through the work of God, the Holy Spirit, who reveals our sins and points us to Christ. By faith in Christ, we shall be in heaven with our Lord forever. It is difficult for us, as sinful mortals, to comprehend eternity with the essence of being forever. If we are fortunate, we may live to be 100 years of age. In this transitory state as pilgrims on the face of this earth, there are problems, trials and vicissitudes to face. The Christian is equipped to deal with these problems in Christ. Paul states, "For to me, to live is Christ, and to die is gain." (Philippians 1:2) "For we brought nothing into the world and we can take nothing out of it." (I Timothy 6:7) Just think of the term---FOREVER----FOREVER---FOREVER.

A COVETED PRIZE TO THE WINNER

During every calendar year, there are countless rodeos scheduled and scattered across our country. They include: Las Vegas, Nevada, Cheyenne, Wyoming, Pendleton, Oregon, Prescott, Arizona, Tucson, Arizona, Salinas, California, Greeley, Colorado, Dodge City, Kansas, Deadwood, South Dakota, San Antonio, Texas and other cities. All of the cowboys participating in these rodeos are striving for the gold buckle, as well as the silver buckle and cash compensation. One thing is sure--- Cowboys, I hope you have excellent health and disability insurance!

The Athenian Games, which were a forerunner of our modern Olympic Games, also had a coveted reward--- the crown of leaves placed on the head of every winner. Just think of the time and practice that an athlete endured to even to qualify for the games. Just think of the exhilaration when the winner reached the finish line. His biceps bulging, breathing heavily, and exhausted. But it was worth it. He won the prize. His reward was a crown of leaves that withered within a few days.

The Christian has a long-range goal; and that is heaven. The world has so many man-made ways to salvation, which are false and contrary to the Scriptures. There is only one way and that is salvation only through the merits of Jesus Christ, as our personal Lord and Savior. We must learn in our witnessing to refute the false ways of salvation and to extol Christ. "For it is by grace you have been saved, through faith---and this not from yourselves, it is the gift of God--- not by works, so that no one can boast." (Ephesians 2:8, 9)

COME HOME!

When we were small children, we loved to play with our friends 'til late in the evening. Our father would call to us "Come, home, you have to get your rest for another day." "Do we have to? We are having so much fun!" Yes," responded our father "Now, is the time to come home!" We obeyed our earthly father. During our pilgrimage, our heavenly Father calls to us as weary pilgrims, "Come home, my child, your work on earth has been completed. Enter the rest I have prepared for you." Heaven is our real home as Christians. This life on this earth is transitory.

> I'm but a stranger here
> Heaven is my home;
> Earth is a desert drear,
> Heaven is my home.
> Danger and sorrow stand
> Round me on ev'ry hand
> Heaven is my fatherland,
> Heaven is my home.

STRANGERS, PILGRIMS, ALIENS

In chapter 11, the writer to the Hebrews elucidates that "by faith," all of the great heroes of faith accomplished the great tasks God had set before them. "And they admitted that they were aliens and strangers on earth." (Hebrews 11:13b) Aliens is PAROIKOS in Greek and stranger is CHENOS in Greek. Most people think and act as if this earth is solid, when it is not. People place their trust in things that are temporal and not spiritual. Paul reminds us, "But our citizenship is in heaven. And we eagerly await a Savior from there, the Lord Jesus Christ." (Philippians 3:20) God assures us that our citizenship (Greek: POLITEUMA) is in heaven. As retired cowboys looked forward in great anticipation to their last round-up on the range, so it is aged Christians look forward to heaven, with the presence of Jesus. The Greek word PAROPIDEMOS clearly denotes a temporary home or pilgrim. We are but sojourners here on this earth. Earth is just a stopping off place; for heaven is our real home. We are pilgrims looking forward towards heaven.

When the church-at-large realizes that Christians are pilgrims on the earth, then there should be a greater urgency to articulate the Good News of Christ who died and rose again for the sins of the world. Have we grasped the urgency of witnessing for Christ? The days are getting shorter. No human being knows when the Last Round-Up will happen.

WATCHMEN

Small, as well as large companies, employ security firms to provide watchmen throughout their properties, especially at night. Although some robberies transpire during the daylight hours, most robberies come under the guise of the darkness of night, when everyone is sleeping. Trained watchmen make their rounds, clock their time pieces to record exactly the time of their viewing of the property. If earthly watchmen are used to insure the safety of property, how much more should we as Christians be watchmen of the ramparts of life. Watch and be vigilant for the souls of mankind!

ARTIFACTS

Artifacts been salvaged from the Titanic shipwreck Titanic have been exhibited in various cities of the U.S.A. and Canada. While on vacation to the Great Northwest, my wife Elaine and I toured the artifacts at museum on Victoria Island, Canada. Every admission ticket had a special number to determine, at the end of the tour, whether you perished or survived. My wife, Elaine, was a survivor. I perished. Many wealthy families, in order not to be recognized or robbed on the Titanic, chose 3rd class tickets. They, like others who were confined to their levels by gates, perished. We never know when our gracious God will end our lives and take us to heaven.

FLASH MOB

At a mall, the "Flash Mob" was used very effectively to advertise the grand opening of the newly dedicated Rijksmuseum in Amsterdam, Netherlands to recreate Rembrandt's painting, "The Night Watch." Rembrandt's painting depicts Captain Frans Banning Cocq and his Lieutenant Willem van Ruytenburch, leading out the city guard, Schutteri. This painting was brought to life by actors dressed in the garb of the 1642 painting. Actors swung from balconies in the mall and assembled at a central place, while a canvass curtain framed them as Rembrandt's renowned painting. This "Flash Mob" incident occurred on April 13, 2013.[3] Just as this flash mob incident was effective and came to the shoppers at the mall, so shall the coming of the Son of Man be on the Last Day. It will be sudden and unexpected!

THE UNSINKABLE SHIP

The sinking of the great, unsinkable Titanic has spawned several true stories during that great tragedy of April 14, 1912, 2 a.m., when 1,522 died. In 1912, Morse Code did not exist. Instead, they used a Marconi system termed CQD. John Philip, a faithful officer who was in charge of communications, sent many frivolous messages for the rich and famous in 1912. He was so busy executing these messages that when the alert came across his wire of the impending doom by the iceberg, he had insufficient time to transmit the message to the wheelhouse. But he did get a saving message out in time for the Carpathia to pick up some survivors.

The people of the world are in distress and sending out spiritual messages to the church to come to their aid. Will we heed their spiritual distress call? Or will we completely ignore their cry for help? As people were herded into the saving lifeboats asked, an evangelist asked as many as he could, "Do you know Jesus as your Savior?" If they did, he asked that they step aside. He had a zeal that the others had the opportunity to know their Lord and Savior Jesus Christ. His dying breath as he was drowning in the Atlantic, "Accept Jesus as your Savior?"

COWARDICE

Sir Cosmo Edmund Duff Gordon and his wife Lucile were passengers on that fateful morning the Titanic sunk. The rule was "women and children first into the lifeboats." As several boats were being lowered, Lucille refused several times to get into the lifeboat. She would only go if her husband could also accompany her. One crewman asked Sir Cosmo to the boat and he accepted. Lifeboat I was lowered into the water with seven crew members and five passengers. There was room for more survivors.

As they rowed away from the sinking ship, they heard the screams of the drowning people around them. When she saw the people drowning, Lady Duff-Gordon told the crew members not to go back to get them, for it was too dangerous for their own lives to pick them up.[4] Here, they ignored the drowning, when they had room in their boat to save them. The crewmen complained to Sir Cosmo that they lost even future pay with the sinking of the Titanic. Sir Cosmo promised to pay each crew member five pounds when they were on the Carpathia.

Later, Sir Cosmo had to defend himself at a Titanic Board of Inquiry, when he arrived in New York City. The question repeatedly asked of Sir Cosmo "Why didn't your boat stop to save the drowning passengers?" Sir Cosmo was very evasive in his answers. There were six witnesses including Sir Cosmo. The American Inquiry lasted 18 days, while the British Inquiry took 36 days. The British Inquiry concluded that Sir Cosmo did not bribe the crew to row away from the drowning people.[5]

But, we are like Lady Duff-Gordon and the crew who were only thinking to save themselves and completely ignored the people drowning. Today it is worse. For people are drowning in their sins and sinking to perdition in eternity. People are spiritually helpless and trying to survive when their Ship of Life goes down. We are saying to them "We are saved, but we can't be bothered with others." Can we in good faith do this? Certainly not. Souls are dying without hope, and without Christ. What are you doing about it? What will you do in the future?

COURAGE

On that fateful night of 1912, the Titanic hit an immense iceberg, that tore a gaping hole in its side. Water rushed in, people panicked, and chaos reigned on the decks of that ship. The orchestra, at first, played familiar songs to calm the crowd. At the very end, they played "Nearer My God to Thee." There were 2,228 passengers on board, but only enough lifeboats to accommodate half of the passengers. 1,522 went down with the ship. The last lifeboat left its moorings at

2a.m. More people could have survived if all of the lifeboats would have been filled to capacity. The big eternal question--- how many of the passengers, especially those who met their Maker that early morning of April 14, 1912, knew Jesus as their personal Savior?

A DAY OF RECKONING

Christ says, "And the gospel of the kingdom will be preached to the whole world as a testimony to all nations, and the end shall come." (Matt. 24:14) We wish on many occasions that time would stand still, for we all have so many items to accomplish in this lifetime. When God's time is ready, then we will have the last round-up of the end of the world. God's messengers, the angels, (not ranch hands), will assist Christ on Judgment Day. The nomenclature Judgment Day, Last Days, and End Times are terms for this event. The eternal fate of every person is determined at death, with the souls of believers going to heaven, while unbelievers are sent to hell. On Judgment Day, we all must appear before the Judgment seat of God. Only while people are still alive, will they have an opportunity to repent of their sins and by the work of the Holy Spirit accept Christ as their personal Savior. A Christian's death is a time of joy to be with Christ in heaven. "I will lie down and sleep in peace, for you alone, O Lord, make me dwell in safety." (Psalm 4:8)

FALSE ALARMS

Many time, false alarms are pulled by pranksters. Although it is a false alarm, the fire department investigates and mobilizes their equipment to put out a supposed fire. There will be no false alarms when God gives the final clarion on Judgment Day. The Scriptures describe the Last Times. (I Thessalonians 5:1, 2; Matthew 24 and 25.) In eschatology, such terms the as the Last Days, Judgment Day, the End Times, and parousia are used.

TEMPUS FUGIT

Time is short and that is why evangelism is so important. We must articulate the gospel and constantly be confessors of the faith until our dying days. Remember, we, too, have to give an account of our lives before the Almighty Lord! Just think---when we are in heaven someone will come up to you and say "I know and accepted Jesus and I am in heaven because you told me about Jesus." There will also be a great joy in heaven. But we have a lot of work to do on this old "terra firma" that is not too firm,; but virtually sinking more deeply into sin. We must be bold watchmen on the ramparts telling everyone of the message of the King of Kings and Lord of Lords.

END OF THE JOURNEY

When young children take road trips throughout our country during vacation time, they become anxious. Parents occupy children's time by playing board games, using their I-pods, computers, singing, or counting the type of different cars. But children become bored. They ask "Are we there yet?" The father replies "Not too far 'til we reach our destination." We are as children of our heavenly Father during our pilgrimage on earth. We become anxious during prolonged illness or hospitalization. Is heaven getting closer?

AN ETERNAL DESIGN

A group of vacationers were touring a carpet factory. The guide pointed out the various looms and intricacies of the carpet pattern. He first showed the underside of the carpet which revealed threads that seemed to go nowhere. He said, "Probably you are wondering how carpet factories can devise such beautiful rugs, when you only see threads that dangle, colors and strings that seemingly go nowhere. Let's go to the catwalk. There, the man in the tower, with his computer, is making the beautiful design." In our lifetime, we often only see the dangled threads, where life has no sense; yet above, our heavenly Father is controlling our lives and developing a beautiful pattern and outcome for us. Often, we fail to realize this. Eternity will only reveal the divine purpose in our lives. We must trust our Lord more. "Commit your way to the Lord, trust in him, and he will do this." (Psalm 37:5)

DAY-LIGHT BREAK-INS

Thieves are bolder today than in other eras. Usually, they strike during the night hours to commit their thievery. This was true when I served Christ Lutheran-Logan Square, Chicago, Illinois (an inner-city congregation.) Our parsonage was located at the juncture of an alley near an apartment complex. We noticed tenants moving in and out. One summer, white uniformed men moved furniture into an unmarked moving van. At the time we thought nothing about it. A week later, a Shakespeare Police Department Detective knocked on our door, asking if we had seen anything out of the ordinary the preceding week. We told him about the unmarked white van. He commented, "Those thieves did it again—in broad daylight!"

On another occasion, our two sons were very vigilant to assist the police to apprehend other robbers by calling the police. The police responded quickly and caught the thieves.

A Mission Director of the Michigan District of the Lutheran Church in Ann Arbor visited restaurants for lunch. One day, he decided to go home instead. As he drove up to his home, he saw an unfamiliar car. Thinking the worst, he proceeded with caution. He let the air out of all four tires on the thieves' car, then parked across the street and called the police. The police arrived quickly and arrested the two thieves who were very surprised by the condition of their get-away car.

These are just a few of the real examples and incidents that happen in everyday life. It reminds us that Jesus predicted that he, too, will come on Judgement Day, as a thief in the night. "For you know very well that the day of the Lord will come like a thief in the night." (I Thessalonians 5:2)

Soon will the Lord, my Life, appear;
Soon shall I end my trials here,
Leave sin and sorrow, death and pain,
To live is Christ, to die is gain.

NOTES

1 Greek for coming, presence
2 A vigilant cowboy would identify this steer to bring other cattle to the slaughter house. A good Judas Steer was used again and again.
3 Flash Mob, *Wikipedia, the Free Encyclopedia*, April 12, 2013.
4 *Encyclopedia Titanica*, Investment Management, Sir Cosmos Edmund Duff-Gordon (Mr. Morgan.)
5 *TIP British Wreck Commissioner's Inquiry*, Titanic Inquiry Project, May 17, 1912. Testimony of Sir Cosmo Duff-Gordon.

"That at the name of Jesus every knee should bow, in heaven and on earth and under the earth, and every tongue confess that Jesus Christ is Lord, to the glory of God the Father." (Philippians 2:10, 11)

"May the God of peace, who through the blood of the eternal covenant brought back from the dead our Lord Jesus, that great Shepherd of the sheep, equip you with everything good for doing his will, and may he work in us what is pleasing to him, through Jesus Christ, to whom be glory for ever and ever. Amen." (Hebrews 13:20, 21)

"Now to him who is able to do immeasurable more than all we ask or imagine, according to his power that is at work within us, to him be glory in the church and in Christ Jesus throughout all generations, for ever and ever! Amen." (Ephesians 3:20-21)

"To him who loved us and has freed us from our sins by his blood, and has made us to be a kingdom and priests to serve his God and Father-to him be glory and power for ever and ever! Amen." (Revelation 1:5b, 6)

SOLI DEO GLORIA

BIBLIOGRAPHY

Adams, Ramon F, Cowboy Lingo, Boston, New York, Houghton Mifflin Company, 1936, renewed 1964

American Cowboy, Vol. 20, No. 4 Boulder, Co. An Active Interest Media, Inc, Dec/Jan, 2014.
Vol. 20, No. 6, April/May, 2014
Vol. 21, No. 1 Collectors Edition, 2014

Barna, George, Baby Busters, The Disillusioned Generation, Northfield Publishing, 1994.
-   Evangelism That Works, Ventura, CA. Regal Books, 1995
-   Generation Next, What You Need to Know About Today's Youth Regal Books, 1999.

Barna, George & Kinnaman, Churchless, Tyndale House Publishers, Inc. Carol Stream, IL. 2014.

Clown Ministry and Wellness, Wellness, Clown Ministry & Faith Formation, 2015.

Constantine the Great, Wikipedia, the Free Encyclopedia.

Gaylor, Dennis, Generational Differences, Springfield, MO. Chi Alpha Campus Ministries, USA, 2002.

Green, Michael, Evangelism Through the Local Church, Nashville, Thomas Nelson Publishers, 1992.

Hamblett, Charles, and Deverson, Jane, Generation X, Greenwich Conn, Fawcett Publications, 1964.

Health Professions and Prelaw Center, Clown Science, Indiana University, Bloomington, IND., 2007.

How, Neil and Strauss, Millennials Rising, The Next Generation Vintage, 2000.

Kinnaman, David and Lyons, Gabe UN Christian Orange, CA. Baker Books, 2012.

Kinnaman, David, The Mosaic Generation: The Mystifying New World of Youth Culture, Ventura, CA, Barna Group, 2006.

Knopf, Alfred, Peter the Great, His Life and World, New York 1980

Mace, Emily, The Nones Are Here... And Has Been For Over 100 Years, Religious Dispatches, January 13, 2015.

McIntosh, Gary L, Make Room for the Boom or Bust, 6 Church Models for Reaching Three Generations, Fleming H. Revell Co. 1997.

Mayhew, Bruce, Multigenerational Characteristics, Bruce Mayhew Consulting, 2014.

Nestle, D. Erwin, Novum Testamentum Graece, Stuttgart, Germany, Privileqierte Wurttembergische Biblanstalt, 1950.

Oppel, Wayne A. The Mosaic Generation: The Future of Christianity? Who Are They and How Will They Change the Future? Winston-Salem, North Carolina, Leadership Advance Online.

Packer, James, Your Father Loves You, Harold Shaw Publishers, 1986.

Pew Research Center, Generation X: America's Neglected Middle Child. 2014

Pew Forum on Region & Public Life, Religious Beliefs and Behaviors, U.S. Religious Landscape Survey, Washington, DC. 2007.

Pew Research Center's Social Demographics, Trends, Millennials in Adulthood, 2014.

Pew Forum on Religion & Public Life, "Nones' on the Rise, Washington, D.C, 2012.

Pieper, Frances, Christian Dogmatics, Volume I, Saint Louis, Concordia Publishing House, 1950
Christian Dogmatics, Volume III, Concordia Publishing House, 1953.

Putman, Robert D. & Campbell, David E. American Grace: How Religion Divides & Unites Us, New York, London, Sydney Simon & Schuster, pages 135-136, 2012

Shaer, Matthew, The Body Shop, Smithsonian, May, 2015, pp. 35-43,

Thompson, Gary, Reaching the Mosaic Generation, The Transformative Church-Making Disciples, 2012.

Tulgan Managing Generation X. How to Bring Out the Best in Young Talent, Merritt, 1995.

U.S. Chamber of Commerce, The Millennial Generation, Washington, D.C. The Millennial Generation Research Review, 2009.

Vine, W.E., Vine's Expository Dictionary of Old & New Testament Words, Nashville, Thomas Nelson, Inc., 1997.

Western Horseman, Augusta, GA, MCC Magazines, LLC, Nov. 2011

Printed in the United States
By Bookmasters